Reading Comprehension & Constructed Response using the RACES Strategy Through The Seasons

By Courtney Bluem
CreateInspireTeach.com

Thank you for your purchase. Please feel free to reach out via email at courtney@createinspireteach.com should you have any questions.

ALL RIGHTS RESERVED

Copyright 2024 Create Inspire Teach

All rights reserved, no part of this book, may be reproduced or distributed in any form beyond the scope of your personal use without the written permission of Create Inspire Teach.

All the materials within this book are the exclusive property of Create Inspire Teach.

TABLE OF CONTENTS

Teacher Directions	9
Student Resources (Bookmark and Poster)	11 - 12
Spring Fiction Passages	13
Wally's Wacky Weather Machine	15 - 16
Luna and the Lost Bird	17 - 18
Pablo's Paintbrush	19 - 20
The Adventures of Captain Bloom	21 - 22
Picnic at the End of the Rainbow	23 - 24
Spring Non-Fiction Passages	25
Spring Festivals Around the World	27 - 28
Spring Stars & Constellations	29 - 30
The Busy Builders of Spring	31 - 32
The Science Behind Spring Blooms	33 - 34

create inspire teach

TABLE OF CONTENTS

Spring's Underground Heroes	35 - 36
Summer Fiction Passages	37
Magic Library Adventure	39 - 40
The Little Astronaut	41 - 42
The Treasure Map	43 - 44
Time Traveling Homework	45 - 46
Jenny's Kite	47 - 48
Summer Non-Fiction Passages	49
The Journey of a Raindrop	51 - 52
Why Bees Are Important	53 - 54
Recycling Matters	55 - 56
Dolphin Talk	57 - 58
Amazing World of Ants	59 - 60

create inspire teach

TABLE OF CONTENTS

Fall Fiction Passages	61
Emily's Magical Journey	63 - 64
Enchanted Pumpkin Patch	65 - 66
A Sweet Adventure	67 - 68
The Pinecone's Purpose	69 - 70
Grandma's Apple Pie	71 - 72
Fall Non-Fiction Passages	73
Fall Leaves	75 - 76
Harvest Parties	77 - 78
Animal Migrations	79 - 80
Corn Maze	81 - 82
Scarecrows	83 - 84
Winter Fiction Passages	85

create inspire teach

TABLE OF CONTENTS

The Snowy Adventure	87 - 88
The Mysterious Snowman	89 - 90
Lucy's Winter Garden	91 - 92
The Cozy Cabin	93 - 94
The Winter Carnival	95 - 96
Winter Non-Fiction Passages	97
Winter Wonders: Animals in Cold	98 - 99
Secret World of Snowflakes	100 - 101
Holidays Around the World	102 - 103
Winter Sports Fun	104 - 105
Dancing Lights of the North	106 - 107
Answer Keys	Spring: 109 - 130 Summer: 131 - 152 Fall: 153 - 174 Winter: 175 - 196

create inspire teach

TEACHER DIRECTIONS:

I know reading comprehension and constructed response paragraph writing can be difficult for students and teachers. This resource will give you and your students a step-by-step strategy for completing constructed responses for informational and literary texts., as well as practice with reading comprehension skills. Each resource contains a reading passage, comprehension questions, and a graphic organizer using the RACES strategy with sentence stems, a writing checklist, writing lines, and an answer key.

Restate the question

Answer the question

Cite evidence

Elaborate

Summarize

How to use this resource:

1. Read the question
2. Number the paragraphs (if applicable)
3. Read the text one time
4. Reread the text to highlight important information related to the question
5. Complete the graphic organizer by answering the question, citing evidence from the text, elaborating on that evidence with your own thinking, and summarizing your answer. Make sure to use the sentence stems
6. Using the completed graphic organizer, students will write their constructed response on the writing paper provided
7. After writing the paragraph, students should refer to the checklist to ensure that they include all components.

Suggestions for use:

Independent Work
Print out the resource for each student to complete on their own either during centers, for homework, or as an early finisher extension activity. You can print the entire group of informational or literary, or choose to focus on one at a time.

Small Group
Group students together to work on the tasks. They can collaborate to read the passage, complete the graphic organizer, and then the paragraph. This is a great opportunity for differentiating instruction and targeting specific writing skills.

Whole Group/ "Teach"
Teacher will model how to find valuable information related to the question within the text. Teacher then models how to complete graphic organizer and write paragraph as students follow along on their own pages. This would work for the first time you introduce this task to students.

create inspire teach

Restate the question

Answer the question

Cite evidence from the text

Explain how the evidence proves your answer

Summarize

PARAGRAPH WRITING
sentence stems

Restate the question

Answer the question

Cite evidence from the text
- According to (title),
- The text points out that
- As shown in paragraph __
- From the text, I can see
- According to the text
- The text says

Explain how the evidence proves your answer
- The evidence shows me
- This proves
- As you can see
- This is important because
- In other words, this is saying
- This shows
- Therefore,

Summarize
- To sum it all up,
- In conclusion,
- Without a doubt,
- Putting it all together,
- In a nutshell,
- To summarize,
- In summary,

Literary & Informational

create inspire teach

Directions: Read the text and complete the chart to answer the question. Then write your response in paragraph form. When you are done complete the checklist.

Name: _____

WALLY'S WACKY WEATHER MACHINE

Wally was not your average eight-year-old. While most kids his age played with toy cars, Wally loved to tinker with gadgets and gizmos. His room was filled with bits and bobs of old machines and weird inventions. One rainy spring morning, Wally decided to create something extraordinary - a Weather Machine!

After hours of twisting wires, tightening bolts, and attaching what seemed like a hundred buttons, Wally's Weather Machine was ready. He had dreamed of making sunny days for picnics and gentle breezes for kite flying. But when he pressed the big red button, something went hilariously wrong.

Instead of a sunny spring day, snowflakes began to fall from the sky! Wally watched in astonishment as his backyard turned into a winter wonderland. He giggled and ran outside to build a snowman in the middle of spring.

The next day, Wally tried to fix the machine. This time, autumn leaves started swirling around as soon as he turned it on. Leaves of orange, red, and yellow danced in the air, and Wally found himself in a pile of leaves, laughing

Each day brought a new surprise. One morning, flowers bloomed instantly in his garden, bees buzzing happily. Another day, a gust of wind carried away his hat, and he chased it around like a playful puppy.

Wally's neighbors were puzzled by the strange weather but found joy in the unexpected. They had snowball fights and then the next day they went leaf-jumping. Mrs. Garcia, next door, even started wearing her sunhat and winter scarf at the same time!

Finally, Wally managed to set things right, and the weather returned to normal. But the town agreed that Wally's Wacky Weather Machine had made this the most unforgettable spring ever. Wally learned that sometimes, the best inventions create not just things but wonderful memories.

1. <u>Part A</u>: What was Wally's goal in creating the Weather Machine?

A. To cause trouble in his neighborhood

B. To make every day snowy for building snowmen

C. To enjoy different seasons in one day

D. To create perfect weather for outdoor activities

<u>Part B</u>: Which piece of text supports your answer to Part A?

A. "Wally loved to tinker with gadgets and gizmos."

B. "He had dreamed of making sunny days for picnics and gentle breezes for kite flying."

C. "Snowflakes began to fall from the sky!"

D. "The next day, Wally tried to fix the machine."

2. What does the phrase 'turned into a winter wonderland' suggest about the weather?

A. It became very hot and sunny.

B. It started raining heavily.

C. It snowed in spring.

D. Flowers bloomed everywhere.

3. Which of the following happened because of Wally's Weather Machine?

A. Snow in spring

B. Autumn leaves swirling

C. Flowers blooming instantly

D. All of the above

4. Find an antonym for the word 'ordinary?'

A. Average

B. Normal

C. Unique

D. Similar

create inspire teach

PROMPT: How did Wally's weather machine help to create wonderful memories for the town?

✓ checklist

Restate the question			
Answer the question			
Cite evidence from the text	• According to the text, • The text says, • It is shown in the text,		
Explain how the evidence proves your answer	• When I read__, I felt... • This part seems important because, • This part shows...		
Summarize	• Piecing everything together... • Drawing everything together... • The big lesson is...		
CAPITAL LETTER, PUNCTUATION MARKS, CORRECT SPELLING			

create inspire teach

Directions: Read the text and complete the chart to answer Name: _____
the question. Then write your response in paragraph form.
When you are done complete the checklist.

LUNA AND THE LOST BIRD

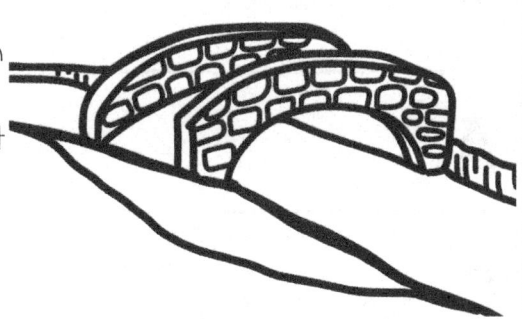

One sunny spring morning, Luna found a tiny bird on the ground. The baby bird, with its fluffy feathers, chirped softly. It had fallen from its nest during a storm last night. Luna knew she had to help. She gently picked up the bird and placed it in a cozy shoebox. "Don't worry, little one. I'll find your home," Luna whispered.

Luna and her mom searched the garden for the nest. Along the way, Luna learned that different birds build different types of nests. Robins use mud and grass, while sparrows like to use sticks and feathers..

They finally found the nest high in an oak tree, but it was too high for Luna to reach. Luna had an idea! She called Mr. Jenkins, their neighbor, who was a firefighter. He came with a tall ladder and carefully placed the baby bird back in its nest.

The mother bird returned, chirping happily. Luna felt a warm glow in her heart as she watched the bird family reunite.

That evening, Luna drew a picture of the birds and their nest. She went to bed dreaming of the little bird and the big adventure they had shared on this beautiful spring day.

1. Why did Luna decide to help the baby bird?

A. It was chirping loudly.

B. It had fallen from its nest.

C. It was flying too low.

D. It was lost in her garden.

2. What is the theme of the story?

A. Birds should be left alone.

B. Helping others is rewarding.

C. Storms are dangerous for birds.

D. Neighbors are always firefighters.

3. How did Luna feel after reuniting the baby bird with its family?

A. Confused

B. Scared

C. Happy

D. Angry

4. What does the phrase "a warm glow in her heart" mean in the context of the story?

A. Luna was feeling hot.

B. Luna was feeling proud and happy.

C. Luna had a light in her heart.

D. Luna was feeling ill.

5. What is a synonym for "reunite" as used in the story?

A. Separate

B. Join again

C. Confuse

D. Leave

create inspire teach

PROMPT: What lesson did Luna learn from helping the baby bird?

✓ checklist

Restate the question

Answer the question

Cite evidence from the text
- One important moment from the story...
- An example from the text is...
- As stated in the text,

Explain how the evidence proves your answer
- This evidence shows me,
- This proves,
- As you can see,

Summarize
- The text leaves us thinking about...
- One thing is certain after reading...
- Reflecting on the story...

CAPITAL LETTER, PUNCTUATION MARKS, CORRECT SPELLING

create inspire teach

Directions: Read the text and complete the chart to answer the question. Then write your response in paragraph form. When you are done complete the checklist.

Name: _____

PABLO'S PAINTBRUSH

In a very gray town, a boy named Pablo found a special paintbrush. This wasn't just any paintbrush; it was magical! With it, Pablo could paint pictures that came to life. He decided to make his boring town beautiful by painting bright and happy spring scenes on the walls.

But even with all the new colors, Pablo noticed that people were too busy to look at his paintings. This made him sad, and he wondered if his magic paintings really mattered.

Then, one day, an elderly lady saw him feeling down and said, "Your paintings are lovely, but people need to find joy themselves." Pablo thought hard about her words. He realized he might not be able to make people notice the beauty around them, but he could teach them how to create it themselves.

So, Pablo started to teach the townspeople how to paint. At first, only a few people were interested, but soon more and more joined in. As they painted together, they began to smile more and see the beauty in everyday things, not just in Pablo's magical paintings.

Pablo learned that the real magic wasn't just in his paintbrush. The best magic happened when he shared his love for painting with others and helped them find happiness in making something beautiful.

The town wasn't gray anymore; it was full of colors and joy because Pablo helped everyone see the world in a new way.

1. Part A: What did Pablo find that changed the town?

A. A book of spells

B. A magical paintbrush

C. A hidden treasure

D. A map of the town

Part B: Which part of the text supports your answer to Part A?

A. "Pablo found a magical paintbrush that made his drawings come to life."

B. "He started painting vibrant spring scenes on the town's walls."

C. "But Pablo noticed that people were too busy to admire his art."

D. "Pablo learned that the true magic wasn't just in his paintbrush."

2. Part A: What lesson did Pablo learn from the elderly lady?

A. That art is not important

B. That he needed a new paintbrush

C. That real change must come from within people

D. That people don't like colorful walls

Part B: How did Pablo apply this lesson?

A. By leaving the town

B. By teaching the townsfolk to paint

C. By painting over his murals

D. By finding another magical object

4. What does 'disheartened' mean as used in the text?

A. Excited

B. Confused

C. Sad and losing hope

D. Energized

create inspire teach

PROMPT: How does Pablo's understanding of joy and beauty change throughout the story?

✓ checklist

Restate the question		
Answer the question		
Cite evidence from the text	• (The character) says... • To support this idea, in paragraph ____, it says • A key detail from the text is...	
Explain how the evidence proves your answer	• I noticed... • Because of this, I think... • An interesting part is when...	
Summarize	• In the end, it's clear that... • Looking back, • It all comes down to...	
CAPITAL LETTER, PUNCTUATION MARKS, CORRECT SPELLING		

create inspire teach

Directions: Read the text and complete the chart to answer the question. Then write your response in paragraph form. When you are done complete the checklist.

Name: _____

THE ADVENTURES OF CAPTAIN BLOOM

Captain Bloom, a kind-hearted pirate, steered his ship through the waves. He and his crew were on an adventure to find a magical island that only appeared every hundred years during the spring season. This island was hidden, but he heard it had the most wonderful plants and animals.

Captain Bloom had an old map that showed the way to the island. "This will be our greatest adventure!" he told his crew.

As they sailed, they entered a thick fog. Not disheartened by the fog, he kept going. When the fog cleared, the beautiful island appeared. The island was full of rainbow-colored trees, shiny birds, and singing flowers.

Captain Bloom wanted to take some of these magical things back with him. "We'll be the richest pirates ever!" he thought.

As he tried to take a sparkling rock, the island began to shake. Captain Bloom realized he was wrong. "This island is not for taking but for learning and enjoying," he said to his crew.

They decided to leave the island as it was, taking only their memories and stories of their adventure. Captain Bloom learned that some treasures are meant to be admired, not taken.

When they sailed away, the island vanished, but the lesson Captain Bloom learned stayed with him forever.

1. Part A: Why did Captain Bloom and his crew go on an adventure?

A. To escape from enemies

B. To find a magical island

C. To hide their treasure

D. To visit friends

Part B: Which part of the text supports your answer to Part A?

A. "Captain Bloom, a kind-hearted pirate, steered his ship through the waves."

B. "This island was hidden, but he heard it had the most wonderful plants and animals."

C. "Captain Bloom wanted to take some of these magical things back with him."

D. "They decided to leave the island as it was, taking only their memories and stories."

2. What lesson did Captain Bloom learn from his adventure?

A. Magical islands appear every day.

B. Fog is dangerous for ships.

C. Treasures are meant to be taken and sold.

D. Some treasures should be admired, not taken.

3. How do Captain Bloom's actions on the island contribute to the story's message?

A. His decision to take treasures shows the value of wealth.

B. His realization and decision to leave the treasures behind showed his learning and respect for nature.

C. His ability to steer the ship demonstrates his skill as a captain.

D. His interaction with the crew shows how to lead a team.

4. What does the word 'vanished' mean in the context of the story?

A. Appeared suddenly

B. Changed color

C. Disappeared from sight

D. Became larger

create inspire teach

PROMPT: What lesson did Captain Bloom learn on the island?

✓ checklist

Restate the question

Answer the question

Cite evidence from the text
- In the beginning/middle/end of the story, it mentions...
- The narrator point out...
- Drawing from the text...

Explain how the evidence proves your answer
- This conversation shows...
- What the characters did here tells us that...
- From what I read, I know this is important because

Summarize
- After reading the text, I realized...
- Overall, the story teaches us...
- All in all,

CAPITAL LETTER, PUNCTUATION MARKS, CORRECT SPELLING

create inspire teach

Directions: Read the text and complete the chart to answer the question. Then write your response in paragraph form. When you are done complete the checklist.

Name: _____

THE PICNIC AT THE END OF THE RAINBOW

On a beautiful spring morning, a rainbow stretched across the sky above Greenwood. Mia, Jack, Lily, Omar, and Emily, a group of curious friends, were thrilled. "Let's find where the rainbow ends!" suggested Mia.

As they embarked on their journey, Jack, who was always in a rush, complained, "We need to hurry, or we'll never get there!" He was so focused on the destination that he almost missed the beauty around him.

While walking through lush green meadows, they saw butterflies fluttering and flowers blooming. Fascinated, Omar said, "Rainbows and butterflies both need sunlight. They remind us of nature's magic." Near a stream, Lily admired the wildflowers. "These flowers are like nature's paintbrush," she mused. When they reached a hill where the rainbow seemed to descend, Jack realized something important. There was no pot of gold, but the scenery was beautiful. He learned that the journey and the time spent with friends were more valuable than any treasure.

The friends laid out their picnic blankets, enjoying snacks in the sun. Jack shared his newfound insight, "I've learned that sometimes, slowing down lets us appreciate the real treasures in life."

Their adventure wasn't just about finding the rainbow's end; it was about discovering the joy in every step of their journey together.

1. <u>Part A</u>: What does Mia propose at the beginning of the story?
A. To have a picnic
B. To find the end of the rainbow
C. To go back home
D. To play a game

<u>Part B</u>: Where in the text does it show Mia's proposal?
A. "Mia, Jack, Lily, Omar, and Emily were thrilled."
B. "Let's find where the rainbow ends!" suggested Mia.
C. "Jack, who was always in a rush, complained."
D. "They saw butterflies fluttering and flowers blooming."

2. <u>Part A</u>: What lesson does Jack learn?
A. Rainbows always lead to gold.
B. Adventures are a waste of time.
C. The journey and friendships are valuable.
D. Butterflies are essential for rainbows.

<u>Part B</u>: Which part of the text supports Jack's lesson?
A. "Jack realized something important."
B. "He learned that the journey and the time spent with friends were more valuable than any treasure."
C. "Omar, fascinated, explained."
D. "Lily admired the wildflowers."

4. What does the word 'curious' mean as used to describe Mia, Jack, Lily, Omar, and Emily?
A. Scared of new experiences
B. Uninterested in exploring
C. Eager to learn or explore new things
D. Confused by the rainbow

create inspire teach

23

PROMPT: What lesson did Jack learn on their journey to find the rainbow?

✓ checklist

Restate the question			
Answer the question			
Cite evidence from the text	• A quote that shows this... • From the dialogue, it's clear that... • The author mentions...		
Explain how the evidence proves your answer	• This made me think of when... • It's interesting that the story says... • This part seems important because...		
Summarize	• To sum it all up, • In conclusion, • Without a doubt,		
CAPITAL LETTER, PUNCTUATION MARKS, CORRECT SPELLING			

create inspire teach

SPRING NON-FICTION PASSAGES

Directions: Read the text and complete the chart to answer the question. Then write your response in paragraph form. When you are done complete the checklist.

Name: _____

SPRING FESTIVALS AROUND THE WORLD

Spring is a magical season that brings warmth, blooms, and celebrations across the globe. Each corner of the world welcomes spring in its own way. Let's explore some of the ways spring is celebrated around the world!

Holi in India

In India, spring bursts into color with the festival of Holi, also known as the Festival of Colors. It's a joyous day when people forget their worries and splash bright colors on each other. Holi symbolizes new beginnings, the victory of good over evil, and is a time for laughter, dance, and sweet treats.

Cherry Blossom Festivals in Japan

In Japan, the Cherry Blossom Festival, or "Hanami," celebrates the fleeting beauty of cherry blossoms. Families and friends gather under the pink and white blossoms for picnics and songs, embracing the transient beauty of life. The cherry blossoms remind us to appreciate every moment.

Easter Traditions

Around the world, Easter welcomes spring with symbols of new life, like eggs and bunnies. People decorate Easter eggs, join in egg hunts, and gather for festive meals. Easter traditions vary, but the spirit of joy and renewal is universal.

The Spirit of Spring

These spring festivals, from Holi to Easter, share a common thread—they celebrate life, renewal, and the beauty of nature. They remind us to cherish the moment, embrace change, and look forward to new beginnings. As spring unfolds, let's carry the spirit of these festivals in our hearts, welcoming the season of growth and happiness.

1. What is the main idea of the passage?
A. Spring is a season of cold and snow.
B. Spring festivals around the world celebrate life, renewal, and the beauty of nature.
C. Easter is celebrated in the same way around the world.
D. Cherry blossoms last all year round.

2. How do Holi and Easter traditions reflect the spirit of spring?
A. By encouraging people to stay indoors
B. Through celebrations that embrace life and new beginnings
C. By marking the end of outdoor activities
D. Through quiet reflection and solitude

3. What does the word 'transient' mean in the context of cherry blossoms?
A. Lasting a short time
B. Happening at night
C. Blooming
D. Brightly colored

4. What effect does spring have on people around the world?
A. It causes people to stay indoors.
B. It causes people to celebrate life and new beginnings.
C. It causes all festivals to occur in India.
D. It causes outdoor activities to be canceled.

create inspire teach

PROMPT:	What are some ways spring is celebrated around the world?	✓ checklist
Restate the question		
Answer the question		
Cite evidence from the text	• According to the text, • The author points out... • This article states that	
Explain how the evidence proves your answer	• This means that... • So, what they are saying • In other words,	
Summarize	• After thinking about all this • When we put all the pieces together, • In short,	
CAPITAL LETTER, PUNCTUATION MARKS, CORRECT SPELLING		

_____

_____

_____

_____

_____

_____

_____

_____

_____

_____

create inspire teach

Directions: Read the text and complete the chart to answer the question. Then write your response in paragraph form. When you are done complete the checklist.

Name: _____

SPRING STARS AND CONSTELLATIONS: A NIGHT SKY ADVENTURE

As the days grow longer and the nights get warmer, spring invites us to explore the twinkling stars and constellations that light up the night sky. Let's take a look at the starry nights of spring!

One of the most famous spring constellations is Leo, the Lion. If you look up at the sky on a clear spring night, you can find Leo by looking for a group of stars that form a shape like a crouching lion. According to ancient myths, Leo was a fierce lion that lived in the sky. The brightest star in Leo is called Regulus, which means "little king," shining brightly as the lion's heart.

Another constellation is Virgo, the Maiden, or a lady. Virgo is easier to spot if you find Spica, its brightest star. It looks like a sparkling diamond. People long ago imagined Virgo as a kind and gentle maiden holding a spike of wheat, which is why Spica shines so brightly.

Lastly, don't miss Boötes, the Herdsman, which looks like a kite in the sky. The brightest star in Boötes is Arcturus. The story goes that Boötes watches over the bears, Big Bear and Little Bear, which circle the North Star.

These constellations are not just groups of stars; they tell stories that have been passed down from generation to generation. As you gaze at the night sky this spring, imagine the ancient tales and adventures that these stars have inspired. Maybe you'll even come up with your own stories!

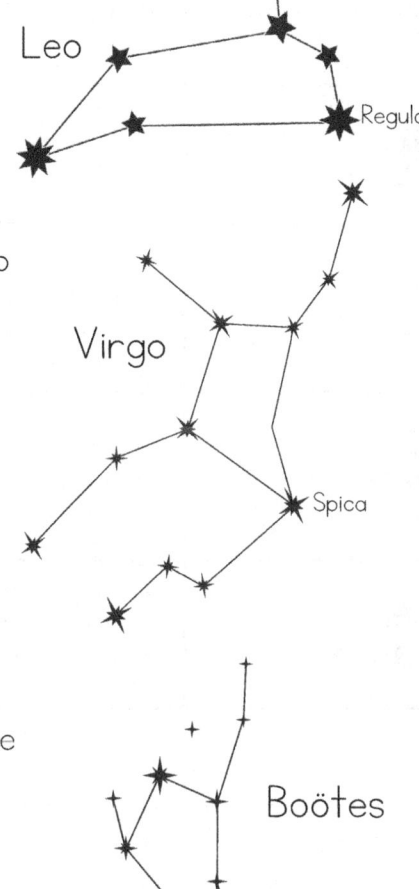

1. What purpose do the stories behind constellations serve according to the passage?
A. To make the sky look more interesting
B. To guide sailors at sea
C. To inspire imagination and share ancient tales
D. To help people predict the weather

2. How are the constellations Leo and Virgo different?
A. Leo represents a kind and gentle figure, while Virgo symbolizes strength.
B. Leo symbolizes a fierce lion, while Virgo is imagined as a kind and gentle maiden.
C. Both represent animals in the sky.
D. Both are related to agricultural symbols.

3. What does the word 'constellations' mean as used in the text?
A. A group of stars forming a recognizable pattern
B. A single bright star in the night sky
C. A mythological creature
D. A type of telescope

4. Which statement is an opinion?
A. The constellation Leo looks like a crouching lion.
B. Spica is the brightest star in Virgo.
C. The stories of constellations inspire imagination.
D. Arcturus is one of the brightest stars visible.

create inspire teach

PROMPT: How did many generations use story telling to understand what the constellations looked like?

✓ checklist

Restate the question

Answer the question

Cite evidence from the text
- Evidence from the article shows...
- The author argues that...
- Based on the text...

Explain how the evidence proves your answer
- That's interesting because it shows that...
- This is important because...
- The reason for this is ...

Summarize
- To conclude,
- This all means that,
- So, the big idea is

CAPITAL LETTER, PUNCTUATION MARKS, CORRECT SPELLING

create inspire teach

Directions: Read the text and complete the chart to answer Name: _____
the question. Then write your response in paragraph form.
When you are done complete the checklist.

THE BUSY BUILDERS OF SPRING: BIRDS AND THEIR NESTS

When spring arrives, it brings a flurry of activity in the trees and bushes. All kinds of birds become busy builders, creating nests for their families. Have you ever wondered how these feathered friends make their homes and care for their babies? Let's find out!

Birds build nests to keep their eggs and baby birds safe and warm. Each bird species has its own special way of making a nest. Some birds, like robins, use mud and grass to make a cup-shaped home in the branches of trees. Others, like sparrows, might use sticks, feathers, and even bits of paper to create a snug nest in a bush or on a building.

The nest is made from twigs, leaves, and grass, carefully woven together. Birds choose safe places to build their nests to protect the eggs from predators.

Materials aren't the only thing that varies; so does location. Eagles, for example, build giant nests high up in tall trees or on cliffs. They use sticks and branches, and their nests can be big enough for a person to sit in!

But why do birds go through all this trouble in spring? Spring is the perfect time for birds to lay eggs and raise their young. The warmer weather means there are plenty of insects and worms to feed hungry baby birds. By the time the babies are ready to leave the nest, the world is full of food, and the temperature is warm.

Chicks grow inside the egg until they are big enough to break through the shell. When they first hatch, they rely on their parents to bring them food and keep them warm. In a few weeks, these chicks will grow feathers and learn to fly.

Caring for their young is a big job. Birds keep their eggs warm by sitting on them until they hatch. Once the baby birds arrive, parents work tirelessly to feed them, sometimes bringing food back to the nest hundreds of times a day!

1. <u>Part A:</u> Why do birds build nests in the spring?
A. To prepare for winter
B. To attract a mate
C. To keep their eggs and baby birds safe and warm
D. To find food more easily

<u>Part B:</u> Which detail from the text supports your answer to Part A?
A. "Birds build nests to keep their eggs and baby birds safe and warm."
B. "Eagles, for example, build giant nests high up in tall trees or on cliffs."
C. "Spring is the perfect time for birds to lay their eggs and raise their young."
D. "Birds keep their eggs warm by sitting on them until they hatch."

2. How do the nesting materials of robins and sparrows differ?
A. Robins use sticks and feathers; sparrows use mud and grass.
B. Robins and sparrows both use mud and grass exclusively.
C. Robins use mud and grass; sparrows use sticks, feathers, and bits of paper.
D. There is no difference; all birds use the same materials.

3. What does 'snug' mean as used in the text?
A. Loose and uncomfortable
B. Cold and unwelcoming
C. Cozy and secure
D. Large and open

create inspire teach

PROMPT: Why do birds build their nests in the spring?			✓ checklist
Restate the question			
Answer the question			
Cite evidence from the text	• The author shows that.. • A quote that stands out is... • As evidence, the passage says...		
Explain how the evidence proves your answer	• What this tells us is ... • So, if you think about it,... • This helps us understand that ...		
Summarize	• From what we've learned, • Putting it all together, • In the end, we can say that		
CAPITAL LETTER, PUNCTUATION MARKS, CORRECT SPELLING			

create inspire teach

Directions: Read the text and complete the chart to answer Name: _____
the question. Then write your response in paragraph form.
When you are done complete the checklist.

THE SCIENCE BEHIND SPRING BLOOMS

Have you ever wondered why so many flowers start to bloom when spring rolls around? After a long, cold winter, the world suddenly bursts into color with all sorts of flowers. Let's dive into the science that wakes up the flowers every spring!

When spring comes, the days get longer, and the sun shines more. This extra sunlight is like a wake-up call for sleeping flowers. The warm rays tell the flowers that it's time to grow.

Sunlight is super important because it helps plants make their food through a process called photosynthesis. This is how flowers get the energy to bloom into the beautiful colors we see.

Temperature plays a big role too. Many flowers need the warmth of spring to start growing. During winter, they rest underground as bulbs or seeds, waiting for the right moment. When the air and soil warm up, it signals to the flowers that the conditions are just right for them to come out and bloom.

Soil nutrients are the food for flowers. Just like we need vitamins to grow strong and healthy, flowers need nutrients from the soil. In spring, the rain helps mix these nutrients up, making it easier for the roots of plants to soak them up. This meal of nutrients gives flowers everything they need to bloom brightly.

Glossary:
Photosynthesis: The process by which plants turn sunlight into food

All these factors work together to create the beautiful spring scenery we love. Sunlight, warmth, and nutrients are nature's way of painting the world with flowers. So, the next time you see a field of blooming flowers, you'll know it's all thanks to the science of spring!

1. Part A: What makes flowers start to bloom in spring?
A. More rainfall
B. Longer days and more sunlight
C. Animals coming out of hibernation
D. People planting more flowers

Part B: Which detail from the text supports your answer to Part A?
A. "The warm rays tell the flowers that it's time to grow."
B. "During winter, they rest underground as bulbs or seeds."
C. "Soil nutrients are the food for flowers."
D. "Sunlight is super important because it helps plants make their food."

3. What does 'photosynthesis' mean as used in the text?
A. The process by which plants lose their leaves
B. The process by which plants absorb water
C. The process by which plants turn sunlight into food
D. The process by which plants sleep during winter

4. Which statement is a fact?
A. Spring is the most beautiful season.
B. All flowers bloom at the same time in spring.
C. Flowers need sunlight to perform photosynthesis.
D. Without rain, flowers would still bloom just as brightly.

5.

Cause	Effect
The weather gets warmer	→

A. A. It causes flowers to remain dormant.
B. It signals flowers to start growing.
C. It makes flowers require less sunlight.
D. It decreases the nutrients in the soil.

create inspire teach

33

PROMPT: Why do flowers bloom in the spring?   ✓ checklist

Restate the question

Answer the question

Cite evidence from the text
- Highlighting this point, the text states...
- From the text we can see...
- Supporting this idea, the text describes...

Explain how the evidence proves your answer
- Because of this, we can see that...
- This makes me think that...
- It's like when...

Summarize
- To wrap this up,
- The main thing to remember is.
- After looking at everything, I think

CAPITAL LETTER, PUNCTUATION MARKS, CORRECT SPELLING

create inspire teach

Directions: Read the text and complete the chart to answer Name: _____
the question. Then write your response in paragraph form.
When you are done complete the checklist.

SPRING'S UNDERGROUND HEROES

When spring comes, not all the magic happens above ground; there's a busy world underground too! Let's take a peek at what goes on beneath the soil and how it helps everything above it bloom.

As the weather warms up, the soil becomes alive with worms, insects, and tiny creatures too small to see. These underground residents are super important for making the soil healthy and ready for plants to grow.

Worms play a big role in spring. They move through the soil, making tiny tunnels that let air and water get to plant roots. They also eat dead leaves, turning them into food for plants. This is a bit like making a vitamin-rich meal for the garden!

Insects are busy too. They help by spreading pollen from flower to flower and keeping harmful bugs away from plants. Each bug has its own special job that keeps the garden healthy.

Healthy soil is like a cozy bed for plants. It holds onto water and gives plants the nutrients they need to grow strong. It also supports the plants, helping them reach up towards the sunlight.

So, next time you see flowers blooming or trees budding in spring, remember there's a whole team of underground heroes helping them grow. Worms, insects, and all the tiny life in the soil work together to create the beautiful spring scenery we all enjoy.

1. <u>Part A</u>: What role do worms play in helping plants grow?
A. They pollinate the flowers.
B. They make tunnels in the soil for air and water.
C. They block sunlight from reaching the plants.
D. They scare away the insects.

<u>Part B</u>: Which detail from the text supports your answer to Part A?
A. "They also eat dead leaves, turning them into food for plants."
B. "Insects are busy too."
C. "Healthy soil is like a cozy bed for plants."
D. "Worms move through the soil, making tiny tunnels that let air and water get to plant roots."

2. How do worms and insects contribute differently to the health of the garden?
A. Worms make tunnels to let air and water into the soil, while insects spread pollen and protect plants from harmful bugs.
B. Worms and insects both eat dead leaves.
C. Worms pollinate flowers, and insects make tunnels.
D. Worms harm plants, and insects help plants grow.

3. Which statement is an opinion?
A. Worms eat dead leaves and turn them into plant food.
B. Insects spread pollen from flower to flower.
C. Healthy soil is crucial for plant growth.
D. Spring's underground heroes make the world a better place.

4. What do worms, insects, and tiny creatures in the soil all contribute to?
A. Making the soil dry
B. Preventing plants from growing
C. Enriching the soil, making it healthy for plants
D. All of the above

create inspire teach

PROMPT: How do worms, insects, and tiny creatures help to get the soil ready for plants? ✓ checklist

Restate the question		
Answer the question		
Cite evidence from the text	• As shown in the paragraph ... • Drawing evidence from the text, • When reading this article, I learned...	
Explain how the evidence proves your answer	• The big idea here is ... • This example shows that • If we look closer, we can find out that ...	
Summarize	• All in all, it seems like • So, what we found out is ... • In summary,	
CAPITAL LETTER, PUNCTUATION MARKS, CORRECT SPELLING		

create inspire teach

SUMMER FICTION PASSAGES

Directions: Read the text and complete the chart to answer the question. Then write your response in paragraph form. When you are done complete the checklist.

Name: _____

THE MAGIC LIBRARY ADVENTURE

Emma didn't usually like going to the library because she thought reading was really boring. But today, her mom and sister really wanted her to come with them on their weekly trip to the library. As Emma was walking between the big bookshelves, she saw a glowing book. She reached out for it, and suddenly, the shelf opened up like a door! It showed a secret room full of colorful books. Emma picked up a book called "Adventures in Storyland." When she opened the book, the room lit up with a bright light, and then, she was standing in a world just like in the storybook.

Emma was greeted by a group of talking animals - a wise owl, a jolly rabbit, and a brave cat. They told her they were characters who lived in this book, and they needed her help to solve a mystery that threatened their world. The characters explained that a fairy tale had been lost, causing chaos in Storyland. Without it, the stories were incomplete. Emma, with her love for puzzles, was excited to help.

Together with her new friends, Emma embarked on a journey. They traveled through different story worlds - from dark forests to big, sparkling castles, facing challenges and solving riddles along the way. After a journey filled with laughter and learning, Emma discovered the lost fairy tale in a forgotten corner of Storyland. The tale was about kindness and the power of words.

With the fairy tale found, Storyland was at peace again. The characters thanked Emma, and then she was transported back to the hidden room in the library. The adventure showed her that every book contains stories and lessons. Emma left the library with a new appreciation for the adventures that lay in the pages of books and that maybe reading wasn't so bad after all.

1. Part A: What did Emma do when she first arrived in the secret room in the library?
A) She read a book about castles.
B) She picked up a book titled "Adventures in Storyland."
C) She talked to a librarian.
D) She found a map of Storyland.

Part B: Why is Emma's action in Part A important to the story?
A) It shows her curiosity and willingness to explore new things.
B) It leads her to the discovery of the lost fairy tale.
C) It illustrates her initial dislike for reading.
D) It reveals her fear of magical places.

2. What was the problem in Storyland?
A) A spell was cast on the kingdom.
B) A fairy tale had been lost.
C) A villain was causing trouble.
D) A treasure was stolen.

3. Choose the correct event.

| Emma initially doesn't want to go to the library because she finds reading boring. | → | Emma opens a book called "Adventures in Storyland" and finds herself in a story world | → | Emma discovers the lost fairy tale in a forgotten corner of Storyland | → | |

A) Emma is greeted by talking animals in Storyland who need her help
B) Emma doesn't want to go to the library because she finds reading boring
C) After solving the mystery, Emma returns to the library with a new appreciation for reading
D) Emma, with her love for puzzles, was excited to help.

create inspire teach

PROMPT: How has Emma's experience in the library changed her view on books and reading?

✓ checklist

Restate the question			
Answer the question			
Cite evidence from the text	• According to the text, • The text says, • It is shown in the text,		
Explain how the evidence proves your answer	• When I read___, I felt... • This part seems important because, • This part shows...		
Summarize	• Piecing everything together... • Drawing everything together... • The big lesson is...		
CAPITAL LETTER, PUNCTUATION MARKS, CORRECT SPELLING			

create inspire teach

Directions: Read the text and complete the chart to answer the question. Then write your response in paragraph form. When you are done complete the checklist.

Name: _____

THE LITTLE ASTRONAUT

Jamie always dreamed of exploring the stars. Every night, he gazed up at the sky, imagining what it would be like to visit other planets. One night, as he looked through his telescope, he made a wish to become an astronaut. To his surprise, a shooting star zipped across the sky, as if answering his wish. That night, Jamie had a magical dream. He found himself wearing a shiny space suit, standing in a gleaming rocket ship. "Welcome, Little Astronaut," said a friendly robot named Astro. "Ready for a space adventure?"

Their first stop was the Moon. As Jamie bounced around in the low gravity, he laughed with joy. He saw the Earth from afar, a beautiful blue marble in the vastness of space. Astro taught him about the Moon's craters and how astronauts had walked on its surface long ago.

Next, they zoomed off to Mars. The Red Planet was fascinating, with huge mountains and deep valleys. Jamie learned that Mars had the tallest volcano and the deepest canyon in the solar system. He imagined what it would be like to have a colony on Mars one day.

The rocket then took them to Saturn. Jamie was in awe of its magnificent rings. He learned that the rings were made of ice and rock. They flew close to the rings, and Jamie felt like he was in a snow globe!

As their journey ended, Jamie and Astro returned to Earth just as the sun was rising. Jamie woke up in his bed. He had traveled the solar system in his dream! From that day on, Jamie's love for space grew even more. He read books about the planets and stars, eager to learn everything he could. He knew that one day, he would become an astronaut and see the wonders of space in real life.

1. Part A: Where did Jamie first stop in his dream space adventure?
A) The Moon.
B) Mars.
C) Saturn.
D) Jupiter.

Part B: What did Jamie learn about during his stop in Part A?
A) How the Earth looked blue from the moon
B) About the Moon's craters and astronaut history.
C) Why there was no gravity on the moon
D) The temperature on the Moon.

2. What did Jamie experience and learn during his space adventure?
A) About how Saturn's rings were made of ice and rock
B) About the tallest volcano and deepest canyon on Mars.
C) About the craters on the moon
D) All of the above.

3. Choose a statement that best completes the chart.

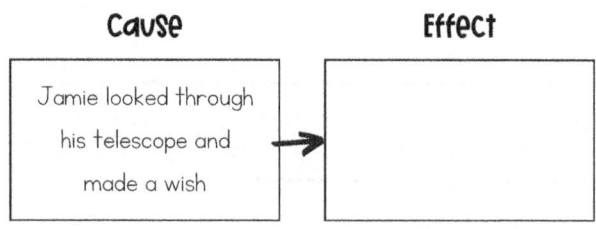

A) He read a book about space
B) He gazed at the stars
C) He decided to become a scientist.
D) He had a magical dream about space.

create inspire teach

PROMPT: What did Jamie learn from his dream about space? ✓ checklist

Restate the question		
Answer the question		
Cite evidence from the text	• One important moment from the story... • An example from the text is... • As stated in the text,	
Explain how the evidence proves your answer	• This evidence shows me • This proves, • As you can see,	
Summarize	• The text leaves us thinking about... • One thing is certain after reading... • Reflecting on the story	
CAPITAL LETTER, PUNCTUATION MARKS, CORRECT SPELLING		

create inspire teach

Directions: Read the text and complete the chart to answer the question. Then write your response in paragraph form. When you are done complete the checklist.

Name: _____

THE TREASURE MAP

Max was always in a hurry, never stopping to listen to anyone. One Saturday, he found an old, tattered map in his attic labeled "Treasure Map." Excitedly, he followed it without telling anyone, not even his best friend, Lily.

The map led Max through the town, into the forest, and finally to a big Oak tree. He started digging frantically but found nothing. Tired and disappointed, he sat down, wondering what went wrong.

Just then, Lily appeared. "I saw you rushing out with that map," she said. "I thought you might need this," handing him a magnifying glass. Looking at the map closely, Max noticed small writing he had missed before, instructing him to take ten steps left from the Oak tree.

Together, they followed the new instructions and found a small box. Inside was not gold or jewels but a note that read, "The real treasure is friendship and patience."

Max realized his haste had made him miss the true meaning of the treasure hunt. He thanked Lily for her help and promised to be more patient. From that day on, Max understood that sometimes, slowing down and having a friend by your side was more valuable than any treasure.

1. <u>Part A</u>: What mistake did Max make when he first reached the big oak tree?
A) He waited too long.
B) He dug in the wrong place.
C) He broke the map.
D) He called Lily for help.

Part B: What helped Max correct his mistake in Part A?
A) A shovel.
B) Lily's magnifying glass.
C) A compass.
D) A phone call.

2. In the passage, the word "tattered" is used to describe the map. Which word is a synonym for "tattered"?
A) Shiny
B) New
C) Worn
D) Colorful

3. Choose the correct event.

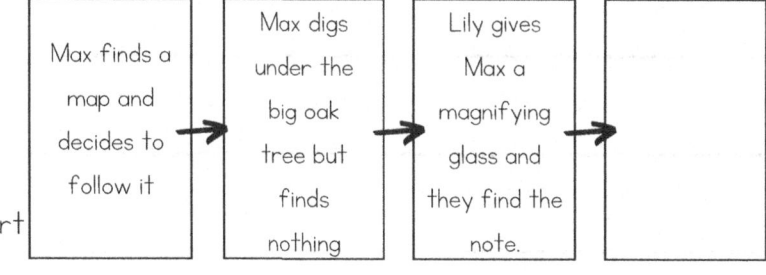

A) He decided not to tell Lily
B) Max followed the map into the town and the forest
C) Max realizes the true meaning of the treasure hunt
D) Max was disappointed when he didn't find anything

4. Which statement best represents the <u>theme</u> of the story?
A) Quick decisions lead to great discoveries.
B) True friendship is more valuable than any treasure.
C) Maps always lead to hidden riches.
D) Adventures are only for the brave and solitary.

create inspire teach

PROMPT: What did Max learn from his adventure with the treasure map?

✓ checklist

Restate the question

Answer the question

Cite evidence from the text
- (The character) says...
- From the dialogue, it's clear that...
- A key detail from the text is...

Explain how the evidence proves your answer
- I noticed...
- Because of this, I think...
- An interesting part is when...

Summarize
- In the end, it's clear that...
- Looking back,
- It all comes down to...

CAPITAL LETTER, PUNCTUATION MARKS, CORRECT SPELLING

create inspire teach

Directions: Read the text and complete the chart to answer the question. Then write your response in paragraph form. When you are done complete the checklist.

Name: _____

THE TIME-TRAVELING HOMEWORK

Alex sat down to work on his homework where he had to write an essay about an important event in history. He chose the moon landing of 1969. As he wrote, his room began to spin, and suddenly, he found himself standing on the moon, watching Neil Armstrong take his historic first step. He was amazed by the astronauts' bravery and the silence of the lunar landscape.

In the blink of an eye, Alex's surroundings changed again. He was now in ancient Egypt, watching the workers build the Great Pyramids of Giza. He admired their methods and the massive size of the pyramids.

The next moment, Alex was taken to Italy, where he saw Leonardo da Vinci painting the Mona Lisa. He saw Leonardo's techniques and the busy streets of Florence.

Finally, Alex returned to his room, his mind buzzing with excitement. He realized that history was more than just facts; it was about the experiences of people and the impact they had on the world. With new excitement, he finished his essay, now with a different perspective on these moments in history. Alex's adventure taught him that history is a living, breathing story, filled with lessons that continue to shape our present and future.

1. Part A: What is the main idea of the passage about Alex's experience while doing his history homework?
A) Alex discovers the fun of time travel.
B) Alex learns about different historical events and figures.
C) History is more than just facts; it's about understanding people's experiences and impact.
D) Alex finishes his homework quickly.

Part B: Which detail from the passage best supports the main idea identified in Part A?
A) Alex chose to write about the moon landing of 1969.
B) Alex saw Neil Armstrong take his first step on the moon.
C) Alex admired Leonardo da Vinci's painting techniques.
D) Alex realized that history was about the experiences of people and the impact they had on the world.

2. What did Alex experience during his time-traveling adventure?
A) Witnessing the moon landing.
B) Observing the building of the Great Pyramids.
C) Seeing Leonardo da Vinci painting the Mona Lisa.
D) All of the above.

3. Choose the Cause and Effect that best supports what happened in the text.

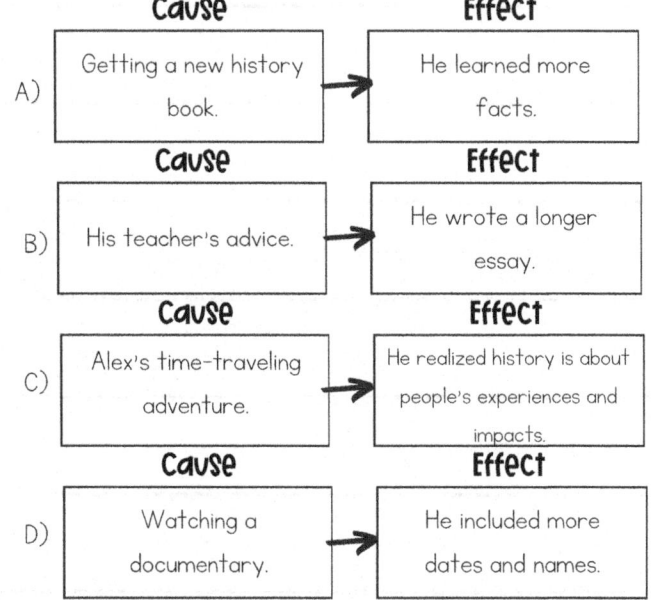

create inspire teach

PROMPT: How did seeing historical events like the moon landing and the building of the Pyramids change the way Alex thinks about history? ✓ checklist

Restate the question		
Answer the question		
Cite evidence from the text	• An instance in the story that supports this idea is... • The narrator point out... • Drawing from the text.	
Explain how the evidence proves your answer	• This conversation shows... • What the characters did here tells us that... • From what I read, I know this is important because	
Summarize	• After reading the text, I realized... • Overall, the story teaches us... • All in all,	
CAPITAL LETTER, PUNCTUATION MARKS, CORRECT SPELLING		

create inspire teach

Directions: Read the text and complete the chart to answer Name: _____
the question. Then write your response in paragraph form.
When you are done complete the checklist.

JENNY'S KITE

Jenny was known in the neighborhood for having the best kite. It was a dazzling blue with a rainbow tail, and it flew higher than any other. Jenny loved showing it off at the park.

One windy day, however, disaster struck. A strong gust of wind sent her kite crashing into a tree, tearing the fabric and snapping the frame. Heartbroken, Jenny grabbed the damaged kite. She was determined to fix it, even though she had never mended one before. The repair was challenging. Jenny had to learn about different materials and techniques. She watched online videos and asked for advice at the local hobby shop. Her first few tries at fixing the kite were unsuccessful. The kite either wouldn't fly or would tumble down after a short flight.

Despite these setbacks, Jenny persevered. She learned to sew to repair the torn fabric and how to balance the frame properly. Each repair taught her something new about her kite and how it worked.

Other children started noticing as Jenny worked on her kite in the park. Some of them had kites with minor damages, and Jenny offered to help, sharing the skills she had learned. Together, they fixed kites of all shapes and sizes, and Jenny felt a new sense of community and friendship.

It was a triumphant moment when Jenny finally got her kite to fly again. It no longer looked perfect, with its patchwork of repairs, but it flew beautifully. Jenny realized that the true joy of kite flying wasn't in having the best kite but in the process of overcoming challenges and helping others.

1. Part A: What lesson does Jenny learn from her experience with the kite?
A) That only new kites can fly properly.
B) The joy of kite flying comes from owning the best kite.
C) The true joy of kite flying is in overcoming challenges and helping others.
D) Learning to sew is an essential skill.

Part B: Which detail from the passage best supports the lesson identified in Part A?
A) Jenny's kite was a dazzling blue with a rainbow tail.
B) A strong gust of wind damaged Jenny's kite.
C) Jenny helped other children repair their kites.
D) Jenny watched online videos to learn about kite repair.

2. In the passage, the word "persevered" describes Jenny's actions when fixing her kite. What does "persevered" mean?
A) Gave up easily.
B) Worked hard even though there were challenges
C) Acted quickly.
D) Asked for help.

3. Choose a statement that best completes the chart.

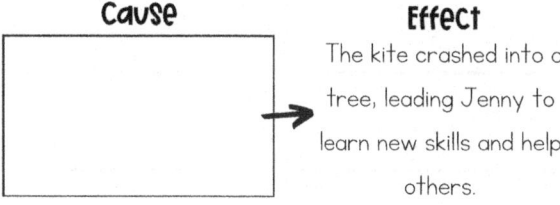

A) Jenny flew the kite too high.
B) Jenny used poor-quality materials.
C) A strong gust of wind came.
D) Jenny had the best kite

create inspire teach

PROMPT:	What lessons did Jenny learn from the experience of fixing her kite?	✓ checklist
Restate the question		
Answer the question		
Cite evidence from the text	• A quote that shows this... • In the beginning/middle/end of the story, it mentions... • The author mentions...	
Explain how the evidence proves your answer	• This made me think of when... • It's interesting that the story says... • This part seems important because...	
Summarize	• To sum it all up, • In conclusion, • Without a doubt,	
CAPITAL LETTER, PUNCTUATION MARKS, CORRECT SPELLING		

SUMMER NONFICTION PASSAGES

Directions: Read the text and complete the chart to answer the question. Then write your response in paragraph form. When you are done complete the checklist.

Name: _____

THE JOURNEY OF A RAINDROP: THE WATER CYCLE

Water is always moving. From the sky to the land and then back again, it travels in a cycle. This cycle is made up of a four steps: evaporation, condensation, precipitation, and collection. Let's follow the cycle to learn how a drop of water can travel around the world!

It all starts with the sun, which heats up water in rivers, lakes, and oceans. The heat turns the water into vapor or steam. This process is called evaporation. The water vapor rises into the air, invisible to our eyes, and begins its journey upward.

As the water vapor goes higher, it reaches cooler air in the sky. When it cools down, it changes back into tiny drops of liquid water. This is called condensation. These tiny water droplets come together to form clouds!

When the clouds get heavy with water, the water falls back to the ground. This is precipitation. Precipitation can come down as rain, snow, sleet, or hail. It depends on how cold it is. Rain and snow are the most common forms that we see.

After the water reaches the ground, it collects in bodies of water. Some of it soaks into the soil and goes underground. Some of it runs over the soil and collects in puddles, streams, rivers, and eventually makes its way back to the oceans. Then the water is ready to start the cycle all over again.

The water cycle is important because it provides us with freshwater. Without it, the water would stay in one place and could become hard to find in some areas. The water cycle also keeps our planet at just the right temperature and helps all plants and animals live and grow. So, the next time you see a cloud or feel raindrops falling from the sky, remember the water cycle. It is a journey that has been happening on Earth for billions of years, and every drop of water has a story to tell about the many places it has been.

1. The passage states, "Water is always moving." Is this the author's opinion or a fact supported by the text?
A) It's the author's opinion.
B) It's a fact supported by the text.
C) It's a suggestion.
D) It's a prediction about the future.

2. What does the word "precipitation" mean in the context of the water cycle?
A) When water soaks into the ground
B) When water vapor turns into liquid and forms clouds
C) When water falls from clouds as rain, snow, sleet, or hail
D) When water moves from land back into oceans

3. What is the main idea of the passage about the water cycle?
A) The sun causes the water cycle to happen.
B) Water travels in a cycle which includes evaporation, condensation, precipitation, and collection.
C) Rain is the only form of precipitation.
D) Clouds are made of tiny water droplets.

4. Part A: What happens to water vapor when it cools down in the sky?
A) It turns into rain immediately.
B) It falls to the ground as precipitation.
C) It gathers into clouds.
D) It heats up and rises even higher.

Part B: Which piece of evidence from the text best supports the answer to Part A?
A) "The sun, which heats up water in rivers, lakes, and oceans."
B) "The water vapor rises into the air, invisible to our eyes, and begins its journey upward."
C) "When it cools down, it changes back into tiny drops of liquid water. These tiny droplets come together to form clouds."
D) "Precipitation can come down as rain, snow, sleet, or hail."

create inspire teach

PROMPT: Why is the water cycle important?			✓ checklist
Restate the question			
Answer the question			
Cite evidence from the text	• According to the text, • The text says, • It is shown in the text,		
Explain how the evidence proves your answer	• This evidence shows me, • This proves, • As you can see,		
Summarize	• To sum it all up, • In conclusion, • Without a doubt,		
CAPITAL LETTER, PUNCTUATION MARKS, CORRECT SPELLING			

create inspire teach

Directions: Read the text and complete the chart to answer the question. Then write your response in paragraph form. When you are done complete the checklist.

Name: _____

WHY BEES ARE SO IMPORTANT

Bees might be small, but they have a big job in nature. Bees help plants grow, make honey, and keep forests and gardens healthy and beautiful.

When bees look for nectar in flowers, they get pollen all over their legs. As they move to the next flower, they take the pollen with them, which helps the flowers make seeds. This is called pollination. Lots of plants need pollination to make the fruits and vegetables we eat.

Bees also make honey from the nectar they collect from flowers. They take it back to their hive and work together to turn it into honey, which they eat when it's cold and there are no flowers around.

Bees are great helpers! They help trees and other plants to grow, which gives homes to birds and bugs. The plants also clean the air for us to breathe and give us food to eat. However, bees need our help. Bees can get sick from too many chemicals on plants or if they don't have enough flowers to visit. We can help bees by planting more flowers and taking care of the environment.

We should look after bees because they help so many plants and animals, including us! Without bees, we wouldn't have many of the foods we like to eat.

1. Part A How do bees help plants?
A) By giving them water
B) By making honey
C) By carrying pollen from one flower to another
D) By stinging them

Part B: What can happen if bees carry pollen to many flowers?
A) The flowers can turn into trees.
B) The flowers can change color.
C) More fruits and vegetables can grow.
D) The flowers can move to another place.

2. What is the main idea of the passage?
A) Bees make honey.
B) Bees are important to our environment.
C) Bees are small insects.
D) Bees live in hives.

3. The word "pollination" means...
A) Decoration of flowers
B) Protection of flowers
C) Growth of flowers
D) Transfer of pollen to help flowers make seeds

4. Which sentence is an opinion?
A) "Bees pollinate flowers, which helps plants grow."
B) "We should look after bees"
C) "Bees make honey from the nectar they collect from flowers."
D) "Bees can get sick from too many chemicals on plants."

create inspire teach

PROMPT: Why are bees important to our planet? ✓ checklist

Restate the question		
Answer the question		
Cite evidence from the text	• The author states.. • In the passage, it mentioned that... • From the reading, I learned...	
Explain how the evidence proves your answer	• This demonstrates that • From this, we can understand that • This detail shed light on	
Summarize	• In a nutshell, • After reading, I know... • The main thing to remember	

CAPITAL LETTER, PUNCTUATION MARKS, CORRECT SPELLING

Directions: Read the text and complete the chart to answer Name: _____
the question. Then write your response in paragraph form.
When you are done complete the checklist.

RECYCLING MATTERS!

Recycling is a process where we take things that we've used before, like paper, plastic, glass, and metal, and make them into new products. It starts when we put these materials into different bins at our homes or schools. Trucks take them to a recycling center where they are sorted, cleaned, and transformed.

Recycling matters a lot for our planet. When we recycle, we use less new material. This means we don't have to cut down as many trees for paper or use as much oil for making plastic. It also helps to save energy. Making products from recycled materials uses less energy than making them from new materials.

Another reason recycling is important is that it reduces the amount of waste sent to landfills. Landfills are where our trash goes when it can't be used again, and they can be harmful to the earth. They take up space and can pollute the air and water.

Recycling also helps to reduce greenhouse gas emissions, which are gases that make the Earth's atmosphere warmer. When we use less energy, we produce fewer of these gases. So recycling helps fight climate change.

By recycling, everyone can help protect the environment. It's a simple action that has a big impact on our planet's health.

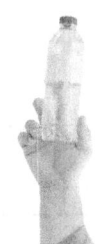

1. Part A: What is the first step in the recycling process?
A) Cutting down trees
B) Sorting materials at the recycling center
C) Putting used materials into different bins
D) Transforming materials into new products

Part B: Which detail from the passage supports the answer to Part A?
A) "Recycling matters a lot for our planet."
B) "Trucks take them to a recycling center where they are sorted, cleaned, and transformed."
C) "Making products from recycled materials uses less energy."
D) "It starts when we put these materials into different bins at our homes or schools."

2. Part A: Why does recycling matter?
A) It makes trash collection easier.
B) It allows people to buy more products.
C) It helps to save energy and reduce pollution.
D) It creates more space for landfills.

Part B: Which two pieces of evidence from the text best support your answer to Part A? (Choose two.)
A) "It starts when we put these materials into different bins at our homes or schools."
B) "It also helps to save energy."
C) "Landfills can pollute the air and water."
D) "Recycling helps fight climate change."

create inspire teach

55

PROMPT: Why is recycling important? ✓ checklist

Restate the question			
Answer the question			
Cite evidence from the text	• In paragraph ___, it says… • An example from the text is… • As cited in the text,		
Explain how the evidence proves your answer	• Connecting this to the question, it's clear that • This part of the text reveals • This supports the idea because		
Summarize	• The biggest idea here is • In short, • All in all,		
CAPITAL LETTER, PUNCTUATION MARKS, CORRECT SPELLING			

create inspire teach

Directions: Read the text and complete the chart to answer the question. Then write your response in paragraph form. When you are done complete the checklist.

Name: _____

DOLPHIN TALK

Dolphins are not just playful creatures of the sea; they are also one of the smartest animals. Just like humans, dolphins use sounds and body movements to talk to one another.

The most common sounds dolphins make are called 'clicks' and 'whistles.' Dolphins use clicks to find things in the water, like fish to eat, which is known as echolocation. Whistles, on the other hand, are used to say hello, show excitement, or call out to other dolphins. Each dolphin has a unique whistle, which is like a name. When a dolphin hears its whistle, it responds.

Dolphins also use body movements to communicate. A jump out of the water can be a sign of happiness. When they slap their tails on the water, it can mean they are upset or there is danger nearby. These movements, along with sounds, make up the language that dolphins use every day.

Researchers believe that dolphins talk about more than just basic needs. They may share information, show feelings, and even make plans for the day's activities. Learning how dolphins talk to each other teaches us more about them and how they spend their days.

Dolphins communicate by using clicks, whistles, and movements, which shows how smart and social they are.

Glossary:
communicate- giving, receiving, and sharing information
echolocation- when animals use sound and echoes to find the location of objects

1. What is the main idea of the passage this passage?
A) Dolphins have a unique way of playing in the water.
B) Dolphins communicate by using sounds and movements.
C) Dolphins are the only creatures in the sea that can make sounds.
D) Dolphins use their tails to communicate different emotions.

2. Why might it be useful for dolphins to have a unique whistle?
A) It helps them stand out when swimming in large groups.
B) It allows other dolphins to identify and respond to them.
C) It scares away predators and protects younger dolphins.
D) It makes it easier for them to catch fish.

3. Part A: According to the text, how are the clicks and whistles used by dolphins different?
A) Clicks are used for playing while whistles are for echolocation.
B) Clicks are for finding food and whistles are for social communication.
C) Whistles are used when dolphins are alone, clicks are used in groups.
D) Clicks are made when dolphins are happy, whistles are made when they are sad.

Part B: Which sentence from the passage supports your answer to Part A? (choose 2)
A) "Dolphins use clicks to find things in the water, like fish to eat."
B) "Each dolphin has a unique whistle, which is like a name."
C) "Dolphins are not just playful creatures of the sea."
D) "A jump out of the water can be a sign of happiness."

create inspire teach

PROMPT: How do dolphins communicate? ✓ checklist

Restate the question

Answer the question

Cite evidence from the text
- The author says that…
- A quote that stands out is…
- As evidence, the passage says…

Explain how the evidence proves your answer
- Drawing conclusions from this, I can see that…
- By stating this, the author is suggesting…
- This is important because

Summarize
- After reading, I think…
- Breaking it down,
- The gist of this passage…

CAPITAL LETTER, PUNCTUATION MARKS, CORRECT SPELLING

create inspire teach

Directions: Read the text and complete the chart to answer the question. Then write your response in paragraph form. When you are done complete the checklist.

Name: _____

THE AMAZING WORLD OF ANTS

Did you know that ants live in underground cities? These cities are super organized and busy, just like big human cities, but they're hidden beneath the ground. Let's explore this fantastic world and learn some cool facts about ant colonies!

In every ant colony, there's a special ant called the queen. She's like the mom of all the ants and lays lots and lots of eggs. There are also worker ants, who do different jobs like taking care of the queen, protecting the nest, and finding food.

Ants talk to each other by using special smells and touches. It's their way of saying, "Hey, let's work together!" Each ant has a specific role, making sure everything runs smoothly in their underground home.

What's really amazing is how ants build tunnels and rooms deep underground. They use these tunnels to keep food, stay warm or cool, and stay safe from other animals. Some ants even grow their own food by making special gardens with leaves and fungus.

Ants are like little detectives when they search for food. They follow scents and use their sharp memory to find their way back home. Teamwork is their secret superpower, making sure all the ants have enough to eat.

Ants also work together to defend their home from intruders and to build and fix their underground city. They show us how teamwork and cooperation can achieve great things!
So, next time you see ants outside, remember that they have a secret underground world full of adventure and teamwork. They might be small, but they're doing big things right beneath our feet!

Ants working together to move an apple

1. What is the main idea of the passage?

A) Ants don't like living together.

B) Ants build tunnels underground.

C) Ants live in organized underground colonies and work together.

D) The queen is like the mom of the ants

2. What does the word "superpower" mean in the sentence "Teamwork is their secret superpower"?

A) A special ability

B) A building ability

C) A type of food

D) A secret code

3. What are some key characteristics of ants and their underground colonies based on the passage?

A) Ants live in underground cities.

B) The queen ant lays lots of eggs.

C) Ants communicate using special smells and touches.

D) All of the above

4. <u>Part A:</u> According to the passage, what is the special role of the queen ant in an ant colony?

A) Laying lots of eggs

B) Finding food for the colony

C) Protecting the nest from intruders

D) Building tunnels

<u>Part B:</u> What statement from the passage supports your answer from Part A?

A) "The queen ant is like the mom of all the ants and lays lots and lots of eggs."

B) "Ants talk to each other by using special smells and touches."

C) "Some ants even grow their own food by making special gardens with leaves and fungus."

D) "Ants follow scents and use their sharp memory to find their way back home."

create inspire teach

PROMPT: How do ants ants help their colony?

✓ checklist

Restate the question	
Answer the question	
Cite evidence from the text • Highlighting this point, the text states... • From the text we can see... • Supporting this idea, the text describes...	
Explain how the evidence proves your answer • Because of this, I think • Putting this another way • This backs up my idea that	
Summarize • Bringing everything together, • To summarize my thoughts • After breaking it down	
CAPITAL LETTER, PUNCTUATION MARKS, CORRECT SPELLING	

create inspire teach

FALL FICTION PASSAGES

Directions: Read the text and complete the chart to answer the question. Then write your response in paragraph form. When you are done complete the checklist.

Name: _____

EMILY'S MAGICAL JOURNEY

In the town of Maplewood, where trees were bursting with shades of red, orange, and yellow during fall, Emily made an extraordinary discovery. On a chilly morning, while walking in the forest, she came across a golden leaf that shined unlike any other. As soon as she picked it up, the world changed around her.

Suddenly, Emily was in the middle of Maplewood's fall festival, but everything looked different. The people wore old-fashioned clothes, and the games they played were the ones she had only seen in history books. Emily realized the leaf had taken her back in time, so she decided to explore.

As she explored, she learned more about Maplewood's traditions. She danced to old tunes, tasted historical recipes, and listened to stories of the town's early days. The golden leaf allowed her to see how the spirit of the festival had remained, even if the celebrations had changed over the years.

As the sun set, Emily found herself back in her own time, still holding the magical leaf. She realized the true value of memories and traditions, and how they connect generations of people in Maplewood.

1. Why did Emily decide to explore the old version of Maplewood's fall festival?
a) She was curious about the historical recipes.
b) The golden leaf had taken her back in time.
c) She wanted to play the old games.
d) The people in old-fashioned clothes invited her.

2. What is the main lesson or moral of the story?
a) Magic can be found in forests.
b) Memories and traditions connect generations of people.
c) Old games are better than new ones.
d) Golden leaves are rare.

3. In the story, the word "extraordinary" is used to describe Emily's discovery. What does "extraordinary" mean in this context?
a) Ordinary
b) Usual
c) Very special or unusual
d) Common

4. From whose point of view is the story told?
a) Emily's
b) The golden leaf's
c) The people of Maplewood
d) A third-person narrator

5. How has the celebration of Maplewood's fall festival changed over the years based on Emily's journey?
a) The festival has completely stopped.
b) The spirit of the festival has not remained the same, but the celebrations have changed.
c) The games played are exactly the same.
d) People no longer wear old-fashioned clothes.

create inspire teach
63

PROMPT: How did Emily's experience at the old Maplewood festival help her understand the town's traditions and the importance of memories?

✓ checklist

Restate the question

Answer the question

Cite evidence from the text
- According to the text,
- The text says,
- It is shown in the text,

Explain how the evidence proves your answer
- When I read__, I felt...
- This part seems important because,
- This part shows...

Summarize
- Piecing everything together...
- Drawing everything together...
- The big lesson is...

CAPITAL LETTER, PUNCTUATION MARKS, CORRECT SPELLING

create inspire teach

Directions: Read the text and complete the chart to answer the question. Then write your response in paragraph form. When you are done complete the checklist.

Name: _____

THE ENCHANTED PUMPKIN PATCH

In the small town of Everglen, children talked about a hidden, magical pumpkin patch. Tucked behind the tall oak trees was a pumpkin patch with a pumpkin that shimmered in the moonlight. The children said that this magical pumpkin granted wishes, but only to the children who believed in its magic.

One crisp afternoon, Mia and Jake were walking in the woods and found the hidden patch with the shimmering pumpkin. Amazed, Mia touched the pumpkin, and it began to glow even brighter. Remembering the stories, Mia and Jake made a wish. Instead of wishing for toys or treats, they wished to help others in their town.

To their astonishment, the pumpkin gave them a bag of golden seeds. Each seed, when planted, would instantly grow and produce fruits or vegetables. With joy and determination, Jake and Mia went around Everglen, planting the magical seeds and turning empty land into huge gardens.

As winter approached, thanks to Mia and Jake's selfless acts, no one in Everglen went hungry. The town was filled with gratitude and warmth. While the enchanted pumpkin remained a secret, its spirit of giving lived on in the hearts of the townspeople, especially Mia and Jake.

1. <u>Part A:</u> What was special about the shimmering pumpkin in the hidden patch?
a) It could dance and sing.
b) It granted wishes to children who believed in its magic.
c) It glowed only during the day.
d) It was the smallest pumpkin in Everglen.

<u>Part B:</u> Which sentence from the passage best supports your answer to Part A?
a) "In the small town of Everglen, children talked about a hidden, magical pumpkin patch."
b) "On a chilly afternoon, Mia and Jake were walking in the woods..."
c) "Amazed, Mia touched the shimmering pumpkin, and it began to glow even brighter."
d) "Tucked behind the tall oak trees was a pumpkin patch with a pumpkin that shimmered in the moonlight."

2. In the passage, the word "astonishment" most likely means:
a) Sadness.
b) Anger.
c) Surprise or amazement.
d) Boredom.

3. Whose point of view is the story told from?
a) Mia's.
b) Jake's.
c) The pumpkin's.
d) A third-person narrator.

4. Which of the following is a theme present in the story?
a) The magic of nature.
b) The value of selflessness and community.
c) The importance of belief.
d) All of the above.

create inspire teach

PROMPT: How did Mia and Jake's discovery of the enchanted pumpkin change the lives of the people in Everglen?

✓ checklist

Restate the question

Answer the question

Cite evidence from the text
- One important moment from the story...
- An example from the text is...
- As stated in the text,

Explain how the evidence proves your answer
- This evidence shows me,
- This proves,
- As you can see,

Summarize
- The text leaves us thinking about...
- One thing is certain after reading...
- Reflecting on the story...

CAPITAL LETTER, PUNCTUATION MARKS, CORRECT SPELLING

create inspire teach

Directions: Read the text and complete the chart to answer the question. Then write your response in paragraph form. When you are done complete the checklist.

Name: _____

A SWEET ADVENTURE

In the heart of the busy town of Harvestville, Mrs. Maple's bakery was known for its delicious pies. One day, two of her most famous pies – Apple Andy and Pumpkin Patty – found themselves side by side on the window sill, basking in the afternoon sun.

"You know, Patty," began Andy, with a mischievous glint in his baked crusty eyes, "I've always wondered what lies beyond this bakery." Patty giggled, "Oh, Andy! Always daydreaming! But I have also wondered about the world outside." As the two pies chatted, a gust of wind blew through the open window, lifting the checkered cloth that covered them. Seeing the opportunity, Andy and Patty hopped off the sill and began their adventure.

The two pies rolled down the streets of Harvestville, experiencing the world in a way they never imagined. They rolled past children playing in parks, over bridges with streams flowing underneath, and through fields filled with the aroma of fall.
But it wasn't all fun and games. At one point, a hungry squirrel tried to get a nibble of Andy, and later, a crow tried to get Patty. Each time, they managed to escape, thanks to their quick thinking and teamwork. After hours of exploration, the pies found themselves on a hill overlooking Harvestville. The town lights twinkled, and from the distance, they could hear the familiar jingle of Mrs. Maple's bakery.

Patty sighed, "It's been an amazing journey, Andy. But I think it's time we head back home. I miss Mrs. Maple." Andy nodded, "You're right, Patty. There's no place like Mrs. Maple's bakery. Let's roll back before she misses us too!" Using the slope of the hill to their advantage, they rolled back into town and jumped onto their familiar spot at the window sill just as Mrs. Maple was closing her shop.

The next morning, a little boy exclaimed, "Look, Mom! It seems like the apple and pumpkin pies have been on some adventure. They're all covered in leaves and twigs!" Mrs. Maple laughed, "Oh, the tales our pies could tell if they could speak!"

As the sun shone on another beautiful day in Harvestville, Apple Andy and Pumpkin Patty shared a secret smile, thinking about their fun adventure but also being happy that they are home.

1. Part A: Why did Apple Andy and Pumpkin Patty decide to leave the bakery?
a) They were not tasty.
b) They wanted to see the world outside.
c) Mrs. Maple asked them to leave.
d) They were sold to a customer.

Part B: Which sentence from the passage best supports your answer to Part A?
a) "Mrs. Maple's bakery was renowned for its delectable pies."
b) "I've always wondered what lies beyond this bakery."
c) "Mrs. Maple laughed, 'Oh, the tales our pies could tell if they could speak!'"
d) "The next morning, a little boy exclaimed, 'Look, Mom!'"

2. The phrase "basking in the afternoon sun" most likely means:
a) Getting baked again.
b) Feeling very hot.
c) Enjoying the warmth and light of the sun.
d) Talking under the sun.

3. Which part of the story signifies the climax of the pies' adventure?
a) When they are sitting on the window sill.
b) When they roll down the streets of Harvestville.
c) When they escape from the squirrel and the crow.
d) When they reach the hill overlooking Harvestville

create inspire teach

PROMPT: How did the Patty and Andy's beliefs change throughout the text?

✓ checklist

Restate the question			
Answer the question			
Cite evidence from the text	• (The character) says… • From the dialogue, it's clear that… • A key detail from the text is…		
Explain how the evidence proves your answer	• I noticed… • Because of this, I think… • An interesting part is when…		
Summarize	• In the end, it's clear that… • Looking back, • It all comes down to…		
CAPITAL LETTER, PUNCTUATION MARKS, CORRECT SPELLING			

create inspire teach

Directions: Read the text and complete the chart to answer the question. Then write your response in paragraph form. When you are done complete the checklist.

Name: _____

THE PINECONE'S PURPOSE: A FALL ADVENTURE

In the heart of Whispering Woods, fall was everyone's favorite season. The leaves turned golden, and the air was crisp. Among the forest's inhabitants was Peter the Pinecone, who lived high up in the oldest pine tree. Unlike other pinecones, Peter often felt out of place and wondered about his purpose.

One brisk morning, a gust of wind carried him away, and he landed in a clearing surrounded by different creatures. Curious eyes stared at him: from a curious rabbit to a clever crow named Clara.

Seeing Peter's confusion, Clara fluttered down and said, "Ah, young Pinecone, everyone in this forest has a purpose. Do you know yours?"

Peter shook his head. "I've always wondered why I exist. I'm not as shiny as dew or as lively as leaves."

An elderly mushroom named Mortimer overheard and chuckled, "Oh, dear Peter! Pinecones, like you, have a grand purpose! You protect and house the seeds of the pine tree. You make sure the forest grows and thrives. When the time is right, you release the seeds, giving birth to new trees."

Peter blinked in surprise. "I do that?"

Clara nodded, "Indeed! And in fall, many pinecones begin their journey, making space for new pinecones to take your place when spring comes."

Peter's heart swelled with pride. With the help of his new friends, he embarked on an adventure to find the perfect spot to release his seeds, ensuring the legacy of the Whispering Woods continued.

The tale of Peter's journey spread throughout the forest, reminding every creature of the beauty of fall and the importance of understanding one's purpose.

1. Part A: What is the main role of a pinecone in the forest, according to the passage?
a) To be a plaything for forest creatures.
b) To fall during autumn.
c) To protect and carry the seeds of the pine tree.
d) To give shade to small animals.

Part B: Which statement from the passage best supports your answer to Part A?
a) "In the heart of Whispering Woods, fall was everyone's favorite season."
b) "Peter often felt out of place and wondered about his purpose."
c) "Pinecones, like you, have a grand purpose! You protect and house the seeds of the pine tree, ensuring the forest grows and thrives."
d) "The tale of Peter's journey spread throughout the forest..."

2. What are the themes or messages of the story?
a) Every being in nature has its unique role.
b) Recognizing your importance can bring joy.
c) Being part of a community helps us learn more about ourselves.
d) All of the above.

3. In the passage, the term "legacy" most likely refers to:
a) A long-standing tradition.
b) An old tale of the forest.
c) Something that is passed down through generations.
d) A path in the Whispering Woods.

4. How did Peter's feelings change throughout the story?
a) He was always confident and never questioned his purpose.
b) He started off curious and ended up proud of his role.
c) He felt the same about his purpose from the beginning to the end.
d) He was sad throughout the entire story.

create inspire teach

PROMPT: How did the Whispering Woods community help Peter the Pinecone understand his importance and role in the forest? ✓ checklist

Restate the question		
Answer the question		
Cite evidence from the text	• An instance in the story that supports this idea is… • The narrator point out… • Drawing from the text…	
Explain how the evidence proves your answer	• This conversation shows… • What the characters did here tells us that… • From what I read, I know this is important because	
Summarize	• After reading the text, I realized… • Overall, the story teaches us… • All in all,	
CAPITAL LETTER, PUNCTUATION MARKS, CORRECT SPELLING		

create inspire teach

Directions: Read the text and complete the chart to answer Name: _____
the question. Then write your response in paragraph form.
When you are done complete the checklist.

GRANDMA'S APPLE PIE

As the leaves began to cover the yard, I knew it was time for our annual pie-making tradition. Every fall, my Grandma Ella and I would spend a day making her famous apple pie.

One sunny afternoon, I went to her cottage and was, greeted by the delightful aroma of spices. "Ready for our pie day?" Grandma Ella asked, her eyes sparkling with excitement. "Always!" I replied.

We started by picking apples from the old tree in her garden. Each apple was a memory, a story of past seasons. As we chose the juiciest ones, Grandma shared tales of her childhood when she and her sisters would climb the tree, competing to pick the highest apple.

Back in the kitchen, I watched as Grandma skillfully peeled and sliced the apples. She then handed me her special spice mix, a secret recipe passed down through generations. "Remember, a pinch of this and a handful of love," she would always say.

As the pie baked, the house filled with an irresistible aroma. I cherished these moments – the warmth, the stories, and the bond that only strengthened over time.

Finally, with the pie cooling on the windowsill, we sat on the porch, sipping hot cider. As the sun set, painting the sky with hues of orange and pink, I realized that it wasn't just about baking a pie. It was about the stories, the memories, and the love that went into it. Grandma Ella's apple pie was a slice of our shared history, and I hoped to continue the tradition for years to come.

1. Why did the narrator look forward to fall every year?
a) Because she loved watching the leaves change colors.
b) To participate in the annual pie-making tradition with Grandma Ella.
c) Because fall was the only time she visited her grandma.
d) Because she loved apple picking.

2. What did Grandma Ella's special spice mix represent?
a) Just another ingredient for the pie.
b) A secret that the narrator wasn't allowed to share.
c) A family recipe passed down through generations.
d) Something she bought from a special store.

3. From whose point of view is the story told?
a) Grandma Ella's
b) The apple tree's
c) A third-person observer
d) The granddaughter's

4. In the passage, the phrase "a slice of our shared history" most likely means:
a) The pie was very old.
b) The pie-making process was a reflection of their family traditions and memories.
c) They always shared a single slice of pie.
d) The pie reminded them of a history lesson.

5. If there was an illustration showing the pie-making process in the kitchen, what might you expect to see based on details from the text?
a) Grandma Ella reading a book.
b) The narrator peeling and slicing apples alone.
c) A messy kitchen with flour everywhere.
d) Grandma Ella skillfully handling apples and the narrator with a spice mix.

create inspire teach
71

PROMPT: What lessons did the narrator learn from making pie with grandma every fall?

✓ checklist

Restate the question		
Answer the question		
Cite evidence from the text	• A quote that shows this... • In the beginning/middle/end of the story, it mentions... • The author mentions...	
Explain how the evidence proves your answer	• This made me think of when... • It's interesting that the story says... • This part seems important because...	
Summarize	• To sum it all up, • In conclusion, • Without a doubt,	
CAPITAL LETTER, PUNCTUATION MARKS, CORRECT SPELLING		

create inspire teach

FALL NON-FICTION PASSAGES

Directions: Read the text and complete the chart to answer the question. Then write your response in paragraph form. When you are done complete the checklist.

Name: _____

FALL LEAVES AND THEIR NEW COLORS

Every year, trees start putting on a beautiful show of colors. Have you ever wondered why leaves change their colors during the fall? It's all thanks to a little science and nature's way of getting ready for the winter.

Inside every leaf is a special substance called chlorophyll (klor-o-fill). Chlorophyll is what gives leaves their green color during spring and summer. But here's the fascinating part: as trees sense less sunlight and feel the cooler temperatures of the fall, they start conserving their energy for the upcoming winter. This means they produce less chlorophyll. As the days get shorter and cooler, trees get a signal that it's time to get ready for winter, and the chlorophyll starts to break down and fade away. When this happens, other hidden colors in the leaves, which were always there but overshadowed by green, begin to shine through!

Some trees, like oak trees, have leaves that turn deep red or brown. Maple trees show off bright reds, sunny oranges, or golden yellows. And aspen trees? Their leaves become a shimmering gold!

So, the next time you see the beautiful fall colors, you'll know it's the trees saying, "Winter is coming, but first, here's a colorful show!"

1. Part A: What is the main idea of this passage?
a. Trees have a special substance called chlorophyll in their leaves.
b. The days become shorter and cooler in the winter.
c. Trees show off different colors to signal the approach of winter.
d. Maple and oak trees are the most common types of trees.

Part B: Which sentence from the passage best supports your answer from Part A?
a. "Inside every leaf is a special substance called chlorophyll (klor-o-fill)."
b. "As the days get shorter and cooler in the fall, trees get a signal that it's time to get ready for winter."
c. "Maple trees show off bright reds, sunny oranges, or golden yellows."
d. "So, the next time you see the beautiful fall colors, you'll know it's the trees saying, 'Winter is coming, but first, here's a colorful show!'"

2. Choose the word that best supports the meaning of the underlined word.
"But here's the fascinating part: as trees sense less sunlight and feel the cooler temperatures of the fall, they start conserving their energy for the upcoming winter."
a. wasting
b. ignoring
c. saving
d. using

3. According to the passage, what happens to chlorophyll when the days get shorter in the fall?
a. It makes the leaves turn green.
b. It starts to break down and fade away.
c. It creates new colors in the leaves.
d. It makes the leaves fall off the trees.

4. Why do you think it's important for trees to prepare for winter?
a. So they can grow fruits.
b. To protect themselves from cold and harsh conditions.
c. To show off their beautiful colors.
d. To ensure they get enough sunlight.

create inspire teach

75

PROMPT: Why do leaves change colors in the fall?   ✓ checklist

Restate the question

Answer the question

Cite evidence from the text
- According to the text,
- The text says,
- It is shown in the text,

Explain how the evidence proves your answer
- This evidence shows me,
- This proves,
- As you can see,

Summarize
- To sum it all up,
- In conclusion,
- Without a doubt,

CAPITAL LETTER, PUNCTUATION MARKS, CORRECT SPELLING

create inspire teach

Directions: Read the text and complete the chart to answer the question. Then write your response in paragraph form. When you are done complete the checklist.

Name: _____

HARVEST PARTIES

All around the world, people love to celebrate the foods they've grown. These celebrations, called harvest festivals, happen when crops are ready to be picked and eaten. Let's take a look at a few!

In America, people celebrate <u>Thanksgiving</u>. Families gather around big tables filled with turkey, corn, and pumpkin pies. They give thanks for the good things that have happened throughout the year.

Over in China, there's the <u>Mid-Autumn Festival</u>. People admire the full moon and share round mooncakes with their loved ones. These sweet cakes symbolize togetherness and harmony.

Germany has a lively celebration named <u>Oktoberfest</u>. Although it starts in September, it's all about October! People come together to dance, sing, and enjoy large mugs of apple cider and other drinks. Delicious sausages and pretzels are often on the menu too!

Let's not forget India and its vibrant <u>Diwali</u> festival. Known as the Festival of Lights, it's a time when homes are decorated with oil lamps and candles. Families come together to feast on sweets, exchange gifts, and thank the goddess Lakshmi for a successful harvest.

Different places, different parties, but one common reason: to celebrate the food that the Earth has given!

1. <u>Part A:</u> What is the main purpose of this passage?
a. To describe different dances from around the world.
b. To explain how different cultures celebrate harvest season.
c. To share recipes from different harvest festivals.
d. To discuss the history of harvest celebrations.

<u>Part B</u>: Which sentence from the passage best supports your answer from Part A?
a. "All around the world, people love to celebrate the foods they've grown."
b. "In America, people celebrate Thanksgiving."
c. "These sweet cakes symbolize togetherness and harmony."

2. Why do different cultures have harvest festivals?
a. To show off their dance moves.
b. To enjoy the cold winter weather.
c. To celebrate the food the Earth has provided.
d. To exchange gifts with neighbors.

3. How do the photos help you understand more about each harvest party?
a. They show what the author looks like
b. They show where each harvest party takes place
c. They show why people celebrate the harvest
d. They show the food each culture enjoys

create inspire teach

PROMPT: How do different cultures celebrate the harvest season? ✓ checklist

Restate the question

Answer the question

Cite evidence from the text
- The author states...
- In the passage, it mentioned that...
- From the reading, I learned...

Explain how the evidence proves your answer
- This demonstrates that
- From this, we can understand that
- This detail shed light on

Summarize
- In a nutshell,
- After reading, I know...
- The main thing to remember

CAPITAL LETTER, PUNCTUATION MARKS, CORRECT SPELLING

create inspire teach

Directions: Read the text and complete the chart to answer the question. Then write your response in paragraph form. When you are done complete the checklist.

Name: _____

JOURNEYS OF FALL: THE MIGRATIONS OF THE ANIMAL WORLD

Every fall, while humans are sipping hot cocoa and watching leaves fall, a different kind of magic happens in the animal world. Thousands of creatures, from the tiniest insects to the largest mammals, embark on epic journeys. This incredible movement from one place to another is called migration.

Many birds, like the Arctic tern and the red knot, fly thousands of miles to escape the cold and find food. They travel from the icy northern regions to the warmer southern lands, using the stars, the Earth's magnetic field, and even landmarks to guide their way. These trips aren't just for a holiday; they're crucial for their survival. But it's not an easy flight; they face challenges like bad weather, hunters, and even getting lost!

The monarch butterfly travels up to 3,000 miles as they travel from North America to Central Mexico during the fall.

While many birds take to the skies, some animals and insects travel by land or sea. One of the most amazing insects is the Monarch butterfly. These insects fly up to 3,000 miles from North America to Central Mexico to avoid the cold winter. Imagine something so tiny going such a long distance! Their journey is made even more magical as they travel in groups, filling the sky with their orange and black wings.

Why do these animals go through such great lengths and face so many dangers? For many, it's about survival. They migrate to find food and to find suitable homes where they can grow.

So, as you cozy up this fall, think about the animals who will travel far and face tough journeys.

1. According to the passage, why do animals migrate?
a. To enjoy the scenery.
b. To escape hunters.
c. To meet other species.
d. To find food and homes.

2. What methods do birds use to guide their migration path?
a. Using the stars.
b. Following the Earth's magnetic field.
c. Recognizing landmarks.
d. All of the above.

3. What does the caption tell us about the Monarch Butterfly?
a. What they look like
b. What they eat
c. About their migration

4. Part A: What is the main idea of the passage?
a. The Monarch butterfly has a unique color pattern.
b. Many animals move from one place to another during fall.
c. Birds use various methods to guide their migration path.
d. Migration is an easy journey for animals.

Part B: Which sentence from the passage best supports your answer from Part A?
a. "Every fall, while humans are sipping hot cocoa and watching leaves fall, a different kind of magic happens in the animal world."
b. "Many birds, like the Arctic tern and the red knot, fly thousands of miles to escape the cold and find food."
c. "One of the most amazing insects is the Monarch butterfly."
d. "They migrate to find food and to find suitable homes where they can thrive."

create inspire teach

PROMPT: Why is it important for animals and insects to migrate during the fall?

✓ checklist

Restate the question			
Answer the question			
Cite evidence from the text	• In paragraph ___, it says... • An example from the text is... • As cited in the text,		
Explain how the evidence proves your answer	• Connecting this to the question, it's clear that • This part of the text reveals • This supports the idea because		
Summarize	• The biggest idea here is • In short, • All in all,		
CAPITAL LETTER, PUNCTUATION MARKS, CORRECT SPELLING			

Directions: Read the text and complete the chart to answer Name: _____
the question. Then write your response in paragraph form.
When you are done complete the checklist.

CORN MAZES: A FALL ADVENTURE!

Imagine walking through tall paths of corn, turning left and right, trying to find your way out. That's the fun of a corn maze! But how did this cool fall activity begin?

In the 1990's, people noticed that big fields of corn could be more than just food. They thought, "Why not turn them into giant puzzles for everyone to enjoy?" And just like that, the first corn mazes were born! These mazes quickly became a fun way to enjoy the crisp fall air.

Creating a corn maze is like drawing a big picture, but on a field! Farmers first decide on a cool design. It could be anything – a giant pumpkin, a spooky ghost, or even a castle! Once they have an idea, they wait for the corn to grow a little. When it's just the right height, they begin to cut out paths. Some farmers even use drones to help them!

Did you know that there are some super-sized corn mazes out there? One of the biggest corn mazes in the world is as big as 40 football fields! And some mazes are so tricky that they even give you a map at the start.

So, the next time you put on your boots and run into a corn maze, think of all the fun and history behind it. It's not just a game; it's a tradition that has been around for many years!

The first corn maze was created in Pennsylvania in the 1993. Now some mazes are created used using GPS and drones!

1. Which sentence from the passage best supports that this passage is about the fun facts and history of corn mazes.?
a. "A long time ago, people noticed that big fields of corn could be more than just food."
b. "Creating a corn maze is like drawing a big picture, but on a field!"
c. "One of the biggest corn mazes in the world covered a space as big as 40 football fields!"
d. "It's not just a game; it's a tradition that has been around for many, many years!"

2. Which statement is true according to the passage?
a. Corn mazes are only made in fall.
b. The first corn mazes were made hundreds of years ago.
c. Some corn mazes are as big as 40 football fields.
d. All of the above.

3. Part A: Why were corn mazes originally created?
a. For farmers to earn money.
b. To feed the local animals.
c. For everyone to enjoy as a fun activity.
d. To store food for winter.

Part B: Which sentence from the passage best supports your answer from Part A?
a. "Imagine walking through tall paths of corn, turning left and right, trying to find your way out."
b. "They thought, 'Why not turn them into giant puzzles for everyone to enjoy?'"
c. "Creating a corn maze is like drawing a big picture, but on a field!"
d. "Some farmers even use drones to help them!"

create inspire teach

PROMPT: How do farmers design corn mazes? ✓ checklist

Restate the question		
Answer the question		
Cite evidence from the text	• The author shows that… • A quote that stands out is… • As evidence, the passage says…	
Explain how the evidence proves your answer	• Drawing conclusions from this, I can see that… • By stating this, the author is suggesting… • This is important because	
Summarize	• After reading, I think… • Breaking it down, • The gist of this passage…	
CAPITAL LETTER, PUNCTUATION MARKS, CORRECT SPELLING		

create inspire teach

Directions: Read the text and complete the chart to answer the question. Then write your response in paragraph form. When you are done complete the checklist.

Name: _____

SCARECROWS: THE WATCHFUL PROTECTORS OF FALL

Long before there were big machines and advanced technology to help farmers, there were scarecrows. Standing tall in fields, with clothes flapping in the wind, these straw-filled figures have a job: to scare away birds and protect the crops.

The idea of the scarecrow has been around for a very long time. Different countries had their own versions. In ancient Egypt, farmers made wooden scarecrows to protect wheat fields from quail. In Japan, they used bamboo frames and old rags.

But why are scarecrows linked with fall? Fall is harvest time. It's when fruits, vegetables, and grains are ready to be picked. And it's also when birds are looking for food. So, farmers put scarecrows in fields to keep the hungry birds away.

Over time, scarecrows became more than just farm helpers. People began making them for fun, using colorful clothes and creative designs. Today, during fall, many towns have scarecrow festivals. Families come together to create the most unique and funniest scarecrows. They have truly become a symbol of the season!

Scarecrows have been used for over 3,000 years. The first known scarecrows were in ancient Egypt, and used to protect wheat fields along the Nile River from flocks of quail.

1. Part A: What is the main purpose of scarecrows?
a. To look funny and entertain people.
b. To be used in festivals.
c. To scare away birds and protect crops.
d. To be a symbol of ancient Egypt.

Part B: Which sentence from the passage best supports your answer from Part A?
a. "Standing tall in fields, with clothes flapping in the wind, these straw-filled figures have a job: to scare away birds and protect the crops."
b. "Over time, scarecrows became more than just farm helpers."
c. "Today, during fall, many towns have scarecrow festivals."
d. "In Japan, they used bamboo frames and old rags."

2. Part A: Over time, how has the use of scarecrows changed?
a. They became symbols of ancient cultures.
b. They are now only used to scare birds.
c. They became part of fall celebrations and festivals.
d. They are considered bad luck.

Part B: Which sentence from the passage supports your answer from Part A?
a. "In ancient Egypt, farmers made wooden scarecrows to protect wheat fields from quail."
b. "But why are scarecrows linked with fall? Fall is harvest time."
c. "Today, during fall, many towns have scarecrow festivals."
d. "Standing tall in fields, with clothes flapping in the wind, these straw-filled figures have a job."

3. Which statement is TRUE based on the passage?
a. Scarecrows were first made in Japan.
b. Only birds are scared of scarecrows.
c. Scarecrows are mainly made from straw.
d. All of the above.

create inspire teach

PROMPT: Why are scarecrows important in the history of farming and how have their roles changed over time?

✓ checklist

Restate the question		
Answer the question		
Cite evidence from the text	• Highlighting this point, the text states... • From the text we can see... • Supporting this idea, the text describes...	
Explain how the evidence proves your answer	• Because of this, I think • Putting this another way • This backs up my idea that	
Summarize	• Bringing everything together, • To summarize my thoughts • After breaking it down	
CAPITAL LETTER, PUNCTUATION MARKS, CORRECT SPELLING		

create inspire teach

WINTER FICTION PASSAGES

Directions: Read the text and complete the chart to answer Name: _____
the question. Then write your response in paragraph form.
When you are done complete the checklist.

THE SNOWY ADVENTURE

Once upon a wintery day in the little town of Pineville, four friends decided to go on an adventure. Wrapped up in scarves, hats, and puffy jackets, they trudged out into the white world, their boots leaving footprints behind them.

Sam, the bravest, led the way with a map he'd drawn himself. Mia carried a backpack full of snacks and a thermos of hot cocoa. Leo had a camera to snap photos, and Zoe brought along her curiosity, which was just as important as anything you could pack.

Their breath puffed out in frosty clouds as they made their way to the Whispering Woods, known for its tall trees and the way the wind whistled through the branches. Today, the woods were quiet, the trees standing like silent, snowy giants.

As they hiked, they played games. They guessed the shapes of clouds and spotted animal tracks crisscrossing the path. They even made up stories about where the squirrels hurried to and why the rabbits hopped so fast.

It was Mia who first spotted something strange: a glittering from a hillside not far off the path. "Look over there!" she pointed. The friends pushed through a bush and found a hidden cave, its entrance sparkling with ice crystals.

They peeked inside. The cave was a palace of ice, with icicles hanging like chandeliers and walls that shimmered blue and purple. Sunlight streamed in from holes in the roof, turning the snow on the floor into a carpet of diamonds.

The friends explored the cave, their voices echoing softly. Leo took pictures, Mia passed around cocoa, and Zoe found a rock with strange markings. It looked like a map or a drawing of the stars.

"We're like explorers," Zoe said, her eyes wide with wonder.

"We are explorers," Sam agreed. "And we've discovered our own secret treasure."

They stayed until the sun began to fade, then made their way back home, promising to keep the secret of the ice cave just between them. But the memories of that day, of the laughter and the glittering ice, stayed with them long after winter had melted into spring.

And sometimes, on clear nights, they'd look up at the stars and think of the cave and the sparkling snow, and they'd know that adventures could be found anywhere, even right in their own backyards.

1. Which of the following statements is true about "The Snowy Adventure"?
a) The story takes place in a busy city.
b) The friends found a palace filled with gold.
c) The friends went on a hike and discovered an ice cave.
d) Sam was scared of exploring the cave.

2. Using context clues from the story, what does 'treasure' most likely mean in this context?
a) A chest filled with gold and jewels
b) A valuable discovery or experience
c) A map leading to hidden riches
d) A collection of rare coins

3. Which character trait best describes Mia?
a) Fearful
b) Careful
c) Adventurous
d) Lazy

4. In the story, the word 'glittering' is used to describe the ice cave. Which word is a synonym for 'glittering'?
a) Dull
b) Sparkling
c) Dark
d) Smooth

create inspire teach

PROMPT: Describe the most important discovery made by the friends during their adventure in the Whispering Woods.

✓ checklist

Restate the question		
Answer the question		
Cite evidence from the text	• According to the text, • The text says, • It is shown in the text,	
Explain how the evidence proves your answer	• When I read___, I felt... • This part seems important because, • This part shows...	
Summarize	• Piecing everything together... • Drawing everything together... • The big lesson is...	

CAPITAL LETTER, PUNCTUATION MARKS, CORRECT SPELLING

create inspire teach

Directions: Read the text and complete the chart to answer the question. Then write your response in paragraph form. When you are done complete the checklist.

Name: _____

THE MYSTERIOUS SNOWMAN

On a snowy lane in the cozy town of Evergreen, the children waited all year for the first snowfall. Not just for snowball fights or to sled down the big hill by Mr. McCreery's barn, but for a special tradition – building Mr. Frosty, their magnificent snowman.

This year, Mr. Frosty stood proudly in the center of the park, wearing a bright red scarf and a hat that wobbled in the wind. Carrot for a nose, coal for eyes, and a big, friendly smile made of pebbles – he was perfect. The children stood back and admired their work, high-fiving each other with mittened hands.

But the next morning, something strange had happened. Mr. Frosty had moved! Not much, just to the edge of the park, but it was enough to cause a flurry of excitement.

"Maybe he's alive," whispered Lily, her eyes wide with wonder.

"Or maybe someone is playing a trick on us," said Max, always the detective.

They decided to keep a watchful eye on Mr. Frosty. Each day, they took turns peeking out their windows, but the snowman only seemed to move when they looked away.

On the fourth morning, Mr. Frosty had moved again, this time next to the big oak tree. Near his new spot, they found a clue: birdseed scattered all around.

"Birds!" exclaimed Zoe. "Maybe they're pecking at the seeds and pushing Mr. Frosty around."

They tested their theory, placing seeds in one spot and watching from afar. Soon enough, a group of plump birds came fluttering down, eating eagerly. But Mr. Frosty didn't move.

The children scratched their heads, puzzled. It was a real winter mystery!

The answer came the next day when they saw Mr. Jasper, the park keeper, chuckling as he pushed Mr. Frosty back to the center of the park.

"You kids did such a fine job, I thought Mr. Frosty deserved the best spot in the park – right where everyone can see him!" he explained.

The children laughed. Their snowman hadn't walked on his own, but he had brought the whole neighborhood together in a bit of wintery fun.

And so, Mr. Frosty stayed in the park all winter, a jolly figure that reminded everyone of the playful mystery and the shared joy that the cold months could bring.

1. Put these events in the order that they happened by number them 1-4.

	Mr. Frosty was moved next to the big oak tree.
	The children built Mr. Frosty.
	Mr. Jasper explained why he moved Mr. Frosty.
	The children found birdseed around Mr. Frosty.

2. In the passage, find a synonym for 'puzzled':
a) Excited
b) Confused
c) Delighted
d) Scared

3. Imagine an illustration of children looking out their windows at Mr. Frosty. What might this picture suggest about the next part of the story?
a) They are planning to build another snowman.
b) They are keeping a watchful eye on Mr. Frosty.
c) They are about to go to school.
d) They are deciding to play elsewhere.

create inspire teach

PROMPT: Why is this passage titled, "The Mysterious Snowman?" ✓ checklist

Restate the question			
Answer the question			
Cite evidence from the text	• One important moment from the story... • An example from the text is... • As stated in the text,		
Explain how the evidence proves your answer	• This evidence shows me. • This proves, • As you can see,		
Summarize	• The text leaves us thinking about... • One thing is certain after reading... • Reflecting on the story...		
	CAPITAL LETTER, PUNCTUATION MARKS, CORRECT SPELLING		

create inspire teach

Directions: Read the text and complete the chart to answer the question. Then write your response in paragraph form. When you are done complete the checklist.

Name: _____

LUCY'S WINTER GARDEN

Lucy loved her garden. In spring, it bloomed with daffodils and tulips. In summer, it buzzed with bees around roses and sunflowers. In fall, it was full of red and gold leaves, but winter turned it into a sparkling wonderland, and that's when Lucy found it most magical.

One crisp winter morning, Lucy put on her warmest coat, a fuzzy hat, and mittens. She stepped outside, her boots crunching on the snow, and took a deep breath. The air was cold but fresh, and her garden was waiting.

She noticed the pond had turned to ice. The trees were bare, their branches covered in white. It looked like everything was asleep, but Lucy knew better. She had learned in school that even in winter, the garden was full of life.

She crouched down to inspect the bushes. Underneath, she saw tracks from rabbits and squirrels. "They must be looking for the nuts and berries I left out," she thought with a smile.

Next, she saw tiny footprints leading to a small hole. "That's where the field mice live," she whispered. "They stay warm under the snow."

Lucy filled the bird feeder, scattering seeds on the snow. Soon, her garden was filled with the flutter of wings and the songs of grateful birds.

Then, she made a surprising discovery. Beneath the snow, she found green shoots pushing up through the earth. "These must be the snowdrops," Lucy guessed. "They don't mind the cold at all!"

Lucy spent the whole afternoon in her winter garden, watching and learning. She saw that every plant and every creature had its way of handling the frosty days.

As the sky turned orange and pink, Lucy went back inside, her cheeks rosy from the cold. She sat by the window with a cup of hot cocoa, gazing out at her garden.

She realized that every season brought its own kind of beauty, even winter. And while the garden looked different under a blanket of snow, it was still full of life and little surprises.

That night, as Lucy snuggled under her blankets, she dreamed of her garden – not just as it was now, but as it would be in the spring, full of color and life once again.

1. <u>Part A</u>: What does Lucy discover under the snow in her garden?
a) A buried treasure
b) Green shoots of snowdrops
c) A lost toy
d) An ice sculpture

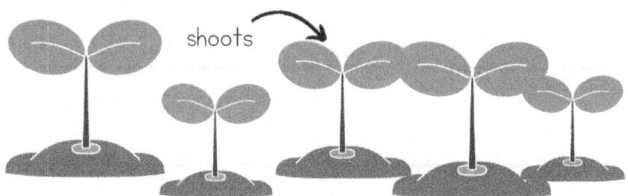

<u>Part B</u>: Which sentence from the text supports your answer in Part A?
a) "She stepped outside, her boots crunching on the snow."
b) "Lucy filled the bird feeder, scattering seeds on the snow."
c) "Beneath the snow, she found green shoots pushing up through the earth."
d) "Lucy went back inside, her cheeks rosy from the cold."

2. In the passage, what does 'magical' most likely mean?
a) Something that involves magic or spells
b) Causing a feeling of great surprise or wonder; enchanting
c) Difficult to understand or explain
d) Something made by a magician

3. What is the effect of Lucy filling the bird feeder?
a) The birds stay away from her garden.
b) The garden becomes filled with the flutter of wings and songs.
c) The snow starts to melt.
d) The rabbits and squirrels come out of hiding.

create inspire teach

PROMPT: What lessons about nature and the changing seasons does Lucy learn from her winter garden?

✓ checklist

Restate the question		
Answer the question		
Cite evidence from the text	• (The character) says... • To support this idea, in paragraph ___, it says • A key detail from the text is...	
Explain how the evidence proves your answer	• I noticed... • Because of this, I think... • An interesting part is when...	
Summarize	• In the end, it's clear that... • Looking back, • It all comes down to...	
CAPITAL LETTER, PUNCTUATION MARKS, CORRECT SPELLING		

create inspire teach

Directions: Read the text and complete the chart to answer the question. Then write your response in paragraph form. When you are done complete the checklist.

Name: _____

THE COZY CABIN

   Miles from the bustling city, nestled in a snowy forest clearing, stood a cozy cabin with smoke curling up from its chimney. This was the Winter family's cabin, and for Emma and her brother, Alex, it was the most magical place to be during winter break.

   Their family had just arrived for the weekend. As they stepped out of the car, the crisp, pine-scented air greeted them, and the untouched snow sparkled. They rushed to the cabin, eager to see the familiar wooden walls and the old stone fireplace that was always the perfect place to warm cold fingers and toes.

   After unpacking, Emma and Alex couldn't wait to explore. They pulled on their snow boots, wound scarves around their necks, and set out to make the most of the winter wonderland.

   Their first stop was the hill behind the cabin, perfect for sledding. They took turns, shrieking with delight as they slid down the smooth, icy path they had created. After many runs and a couple of friendly snowball fights, they decided to build a snowman. They rolled big snowballs for the body and found rocks for eyes, a carrot for the nose, and sticks for arms. He was a great snowman.

   As dusk fell, the temperature dropped, and the children headed inside, noses red and cheeks flushed from the cold. Inside, the cabin was warm and inviting. Their parents had started a fire, and the flames danced merrily in the fireplace.

   That evening, they all sat by the fire, sipping hot chocolate and sharing stories. The cabin was filled with the sound of laughter and the comforting crackle of the firewood. Emma and Alex felt cozy and safe, wrapped in the soft glow of the firelight.

   The next day brought more adventures. They found animal tracks in the snow and followed them, pretending to be explorers. They discovered a family of deer grazing quietly, and for a moment, everything was still.

   Back at the cabin, their parents had made a warm, delicious meal. The family sat around the table, sharing their day's adventures and planning the next. There were more hills to sled down, more snowmen to build, and perhaps even ice-skating on the frozen pond nearby.

   When the weekend came to an end, Emma and Alex were sad to leave the cabin. But as they drove away, they knew they would carry the warmth of the cabin with them, not just in their memories, but in their hearts, long after the snow had melted and the first blooms of spring had appeared.

   The Cozy Cabin was more than just a place; it was a reminder that the simplest moments are the most precious.

1. <u>Part A:</u> What did Emma and Alex first do when they arrived at the cabin?
a) Built a snowman
b) Drank hot chocolate
c) Went sledding
d) Sat by the fireplace

<u>Part B:</u> Which sentence from the text supports your answer in Part A?
a) "They pulled on their snow boots, wound scarves around their necks, and set out to make the most of the winter wonderland."
b) "Inside, the cabin was warm and inviting."
c) "They rolled big snowballs for the body and found rocks for eyes, a carrot for the nose, and sticks for arms."
d) "Their first stop was the hill behind the cabin, perfect for sledding."

2. What does 'bustling' most likely mean in the context of the story?
a) Quiet and calm
b) Busy and lively
c) Slow and dull
d) Cold and snowy

create inspire teach

PROMPT: Why did Emma and Alex enjoy their time at the cabin? ✓ checklist

Restate the question

Answer the question

Cite evidence from the text
- In the beginning/middle/end of the story, it mentions...
- The narrator point out...
- Drawing from the text.

Explain how the evidence proves your answer
- This conversation shows...
- What the characters did here tells us that...
- From what I read, I know this is important because

Summarize
- After reading the text, I realized...
- Overall, the story teaches us...
- All in all,

CAPITAL LETTER, PUNCTUATION MARKS, CORRECT SPELLING

create inspire teach

Directions: Read the text and complete the chart to answer the question. Then write your response in paragraph form. When you are done complete the checklist.

Name: _____

THE WINTER CARNIVAL AT SUNNYVALE SCHOOL

One chilly winter day, Sunnyvale School was buzzing with excitement. Today was the day of the Winter Carnival, and everyone was ready for fun!

The school was transformed into a winter wonderland. Colorful banners swayed in the breeze, and laughter filled the air. There were games like 'Snowball Toss' and 'Find the Penguin,' and a big slide made of snow!

Mrs. Lee's 2nd-grade class was in charge of the 'Hot Chocolate Stand.' Tommy, Sara, and their friends had worked together to set it up. They had big jugs of hot chocolate and piles of marshmallows.

"Remember, teamwork makes our stand the best!" Mrs. Lee reminded them with a smile.

At the snowball toss, children lined up to throw snowballs at targets. Each time someone hit the bullseye, everyone cheered. It didn't matter if it was a hit or a miss; everyone was having a great time.

Nearby, the 'Find the Penguin' game was a big hit. Children searched for hidden penguin toys around the playground. "I found one!" yelled Max, holding up a small toy penguin. His friends gathered around, clapping and laughing.

At the hot chocolate stand, Tommy and Sara worked together. Tommy poured the hot chocolate, and Sara added the marshmallows. "Teamwork is fun!" Sara said, giggling as she handed a cup to a little kindergartener.

As the day went on, children slid down the snow slide, laughing and squealing with joy. Even the teachers took turns, sliding down with big smiles.

The Winter Carnival wasn't just about winning games or drinking hot chocolate. It was about being together, helping each other, and enjoying the day as a community.

When the sun began to set, and the carnival came to an end, the children felt happy and tired. They had learned that working together and sharing joy made everything more fun.

As they left the schoolyard, the lights from the carnival twinkled like stars. They waved goodbye, already looking forward to next year's Winter Carnival.

That night, as the children of Sunnyvale School drifted off to sleep, they dreamt of snowflakes, laughter, and the warmth of friendship.

1. Put these events in the order that they happened by number them 1-4.

	Tommy and Sara worked together at the Hot Chocolate Stand.
	The children felt happy and tired at the end of the day.
	The schoolyard was turned into a winter wonderland.
	Children searched for hidden penguin toys.

2. What mood is created during the Winter Carnival?
a) Mysterious
b) Exciting and joyful
c) Scary
d) Sad

3. Imagine an illustration showing children playing the 'Snowball Toss' game. How does this image relate to the story?
a) It shows the competitive nature of the carnival.
b) It reflects the fun and community spirit of the carnival.
c) It indicates that the story is about sports.
d) It suggests that the carnival was held indoors.

create inspire teach

PROMPT: How did teamwork make the winter carnival successful? ✓ checklist

Restate the question			
Answer the question			
Cite evidence from the text	• A quote that shows this... • From the dialogue, it's clear that... • The author mentions...		
Explain how the evidence proves your answer	• This made me think of when... • It's interesting that the story says... • This part seems important because...		
Summarize	• To sum it all up, • In conclusion, • Without a doubt,		
CAPITAL LETTER, PUNCTUATION MARKS, CORRECT SPELLING			

create inspire teach

WINTER NON-FICTION PASSAGES

Directions: Read the text and complete the chart to answer the question. Then write your response in paragraph form. When you are done complete the checklist.

Name: _____

WINTER WONDERS: ANIMALS IN THE COLD

Did you know that animals have special ways to survive the cold winter? Let's explore some amazing winter adaptations!

Bears are famous for hibernating. When it gets cold, they find a cozy den and take a long sleep. Their heartbeats slow down, and they use their fat stores for energy. This way, they don't need to eat until spring!

Meanwhile, some birds, like geese, fly to warmer places. This journey is called migration. They travel long distances to find food and a warm habitat.

But what about the tiny squirrels? They don't hibernate or migrate. Instead, they collect nuts in the fall and hide them. During winter, they use these hidden treasures as their food supply.

Each of these animals has a special way to handle the chilly weather. While we bundle up in coats and scarves, they use their own amazing methods to enjoy the winter wonderland!

Geese are born with the instinct to migrate. They don't learn it from their parents; they are naturally programmed to know when and where to go.

1. <u>Part A:</u> What is the main idea of this passage?
a) Bears are the most interesting animals in winter.
b) Different animals have unique ways to survive in winter.
c) Squirrels are smarter than other animals in winter.
d) Birds migrate every season, not just in winter.

<u>Part B:</u> Which sentence from the passage best supports your answer to Part A?
a) "When it gets cold, bears find a cozy den and take a long sleep.
b) Birds travel long distances to find food and a warm habitat.
c) Squirrels use these hidden treasures as their food supply.
d) Each of these animals has a special way to handle the chilly weather."

2. What is the synonym of 'hibernating' as used in the passage?
a) Sleeping
b) Eating
c) Migrating
d) Playing

3. If there was a sidebar in the passage about 'migration,' what information would it most likely contain?
a) Different types of nuts squirrels eat.
b) The process of bears falling asleep.
c) Why some birds fly to warmer places in winter.
d) How animals play in the snow.

4. If you read another text about animals in summer, what detail would most likely be different compared to this passage?
a) Bears hibernating
b) Birds migrating
c) Squirrels storing food
d) All of the above

create inspire teach

PROMPT: How do animals do to survive in the winter? ✓ checklist

Restate the question			
Answer the question			
Cite evidence from the text	• According to the text, • The text says, • It is shown in the text,		
Explain how the evidence proves your answer	• This evidence shows me, • This proves, • As you can see,		
Summarize	• To sum it all up, • In conclusion, • Without a doubt,		
	CAPITAL LETTER, PUNCTUATION MARKS, CORRECT SPELLING		

create inspire teach

Directions: Read the text and complete the chart to answer the question. Then write your response in paragraph form. When you are done complete the checklist.

Name: _____

THE SECRET WORLD OF SNOWFLAKES

Have you ever caught a snowflake on your glove and looked at its tiny, beautiful shape? Every snowflake is a small wonder of nature. Let's discover how they are made!

Snowflakes begin their life high up in the cold sky. When it's very cold, tiny drops of water in clouds freeze into ice crystals. As these crystals fall through the sky, they bump into each other and stick together. This journey is like a dance where they collect more and more tiny ice pieces.

The most amazing part is that each snowflake takes its own path. Because they travel different ways, they look different too. It's like each snowflake has its own story to tell. That's why no two snowflakes are exactly alike!

Some snowflakes might look like stars, others like tiny needles, and some even look like beautiful lace. So next time it snows, catch a flake and take a close look. You'll be holding a unique piece of winter's magic in your hand!

1. Part A: According to the passage, how are snowflakes formed?
a) From raindrops freezing in the sky.
b) By clouds moving in the sky.
c) From tiny drops of water freezing into ice crystals in clouds.
d) From snow falling and sticking together on the ground.

Part B: Which detail from the passage supports your answer in Part A?
a) "Every snowflake is a small wonder of nature."
b) "Snowflakes begin their life high up in the cold sky."
c) "Some snowflakes might look like stars, others like tiny needles."
d) "You'll be holding a unique piece of winter's magic in your hand."

2. What sequence best describes the formation of a snowflake as explained in the text?
a) It freezes, falls, bumps into other crystals, sticks together.
b) It bumps into other crystals, sticks together, freezes, falls.
c) It falls, bumps into other crystals, freezes, sticks together.
d) It sticks together, falls, bumps into other crystals, freezes.

3. What is an antonym of 'unique' as used in the passage?
a) Special
b) Ordinary
c) Beautiful
d) Rare

4. If you were to add a diagram to this passage, what would it most likely show?
a) How animals live in the snow.
b) The process of a snowflake's formation.
c) Different types of winter sports.
d) How to catch snowflakes on a glove.

create inspire teach

PROMPT: Why doesn't every snowflake look the same?			✓ checklist
Restate the question			
Answer the question			
Cite evidence from the text	• In paragraph ___, it says... • An example from the text is... • As cited in the text,		
Explain how the evidence proves your answer	• Connecting this to the question, it's clear that • This part of the text reveals • This supports the idea because		
Summarize	• The biggest idea here is • In short, • All in all,		
CAPITAL LETTER, PUNCTUATION MARKS, CORRECT SPELLING			

create inspire teach

Directions: Read the text and complete the chart to answer the question. Then write your response in paragraph form. When you are done complete the checklist.

Name: _____

WINTER HOLIDAYS AROUND THE WORLD

Winter is a time of joy and celebration around the globe. Different countries have unique holidays with exciting traditions!

In the United States, people celebrate Christmas by decorating trees and exchanging gifts. Families gather to share meals and enjoy the <u>festive</u> spirit.

Far away in India, there's a festival called Diwali. It's a festival of lights where people light lamps, set off fireworks, and eat delicious sweets. It symbolizes the victory of light over darkness.

In Mexico, families celebrate Las Posadas. For nine nights, they reenact Mary and Joseph's journey to Bethlehem with songs and processions. Piñatas filled with treats add fun to the celebration.

Hanukkah, a Jewish holiday, is celebrated with the lighting of the menorah, a special candle holder. Families enjoy games and foods fried in oil, like latkes and doughnuts.

Each of these holidays brings people together. They remind us of kindness, sharing, and the beauty of different cultures during the magical winter season.

1. What is a common theme in all the winter holidays mentioned in the passage?
a) Giving and receiving gifts.
b) Decorating homes and public places.
c) Celebrating with food and traditions.
d) Spending time outdoors in the snow.

2. Which holiday is celebrated with a specific activity for nine nights?
a) Christmas in the United States.
b) Diwali in India.
c) Las Posadas in Mexico.
d) Hanukkah.

3. What does 'festival' most closely mean in this context?
a) A large meal.
b) A religious ceremony.
c) A celebration or gathering with special activities.
d) A public speech or announcement.

4. If you read another text about summer holidays, what detail would most likely be different compared to this passage?
a) The type of celebrations.
b) The seasonal activities.
c) The cultural significance of the holidays.
d) All of the above.

create inspire teach

PROMPT: What are some winter holidays celebrated around the world, and how are they celebrated?

✓ checklist

Restate the question		
Answer the question		
Cite evidence from the text	• The author shows that... • A quote that stands out is... • As evidence, the passage says...	
Explain how the evidence proves your answer	• Drawing conclusions from this, I can see that... • By stating this, the author is suggesting... • This is important because	
Summarize	• After reading, I think... • Breaking it down, • The gist of this passage...	
CAPITAL LETTER, PUNCTUATION MARKS, CORRECT SPELLING		

create inspire teach

Directions: Read the text and complete the chart to answer Name: _____
the question. Then write your response in paragraph form.
When you are done complete the checklist.

WINTER SPORTS FUN

Winter is a season of fun and games, especially with winter sports! Have you ever watched skiing, snowboarding, or ice skating? These sports are not just exciting to watch but also <u>thrilling</u> to play.

Skiing is a sport where people slide down snowy hills on skis. It has been around for thousands of years. Originally, skis were used to travel over snow in cold countries. Now, skiing is a popular winter sport all over the world.

Snowboarding is like skiing, but instead of two skis, you use one big board. Did you know snowboarding started in the 1960s? It was inspired by surfing and skateboarding. People loved the idea of surfing on snow!

Ice skating is gliding on ice with skates. It's been around for centuries and began as a way to move across frozen lakes and rivers. Today, ice skating is a favorite winter activity. Some people even dance on ice!

Each of these sports is special. They remind us of the joy and excitement of winter. Maybe one day, you'll try one of them too!

1. <u>Part A:</u> What is the main idea of the passage?
a) Ice skating is the oldest winter sport.
b) Winter sports include skiing, snowboarding, and ice skating.
c) Snowboarding is the most popular winter sport.
d) Winter is the only time to play sports.

<u>Part B:</u> Which detail from the passage supports your answer in Part A?
a) "Skiing is a sport where people slide down snowy hills on skis."
b) "Snowboarding started in the 1960s."
c) "Ice skating is gliding on ice with skates."
d) "Each of these sports is special."

3. What is the synonym of 'thrilling' as used in the passage?
a) Scary
b) Exciting
c) Slow
d) Boring

4. What effect did the invention of snowboarding have on winter sports?
a) It made skiing less popular.
b) It added a new, exciting option inspired by surfing and skateboarding.
c) It replaced ice skating.
d) It changed the way skiing was performed.

2. Match the winter sport with its historical origin:

Skiing	Began as a way to move across frozen lakes and rivers.
Snowboarding	Used for travel over snow in cold countries thousands of years ago.
Ice Skating	Inspired by surfing and skateboarding, started in the 1960s.

create inspire teach

PROMPT:	Explain how winter sports like skiing, snowboarding, and ice skating have changed over time.	✓ checklist
Restate the question		
Answer the question		
Cite evidence from the text	• Highlighting this point, the text states… • From the text we can see… • Supporting this idea, the text describes…	
Explain how the evidence proves your answer	• Because of this, I think • Putting this another way • This backs up my idea that	
Summarize	• Bringing everything together, • To summarize my thoughts • After breaking it down,	
	CAPITAL LETTER, PUNCTUATION MARKS, CORRECT SPELLING	

create inspire teach

Directions: Read the text and complete the chart to answer the question. Then write your response in paragraph form. When you are done complete the checklist.

Name: _____

THE DANCING LIGHTS OF THE NORTH

Have you ever seen pictures of bright, colorful lights in the night sky? Those are the Aurora Borealis, also known as the Northern Lights. They look like magical ribbons waving in the sky. But what causes these beautiful lights?

The sun sends out tiny particles that travel through space. When these particles reach the Earth, they meet our planet's magnetic field. The North and South Poles have strong magnetic forces. So, these particles are pulled towards them. When these particles from the sun touch the gases in the Earth's atmosphere, they light up! It's like nature's own light show!

The colors of the Northern Lights can be green, pink, purple, blue, and even red. They dance in the sky, especially during long, dark nights. The best places to see them is near the North Pole, in countries like Canada, Norway, and Iceland. People travel from all over the world to see this display. The Northern Lights remind us how beautiful and mysterious our planet can be.

1. Part A: What is the main idea of this passage?
a) The Northern Lights are a light show caused by the sun's particles.
b) The Northern Lights can only be seen in Canada, Norway, and Iceland.
c) The Northern Lights are always green in color.
d) The sun is the only star that affects Earth.

Part B: Which detail from the passage supports your answer in Part A?
a) "They look like magical ribbons waving in the sky."
b) "When these particles from the sun touch the gases in the Earth's atmosphere, they light up!"
c) "The best places to see them are near the North Pole."
d) "They dance in the sky, especially during long, dark nights."

3. How do the Northern Lights form, according to the passage?
<u>a) The Earth's atmosphere creates them on its own.</u>
<u>b) The sun's particles reach Earth and light up when they touch atmospheric gases.</u>
c) They are caused by the moon reflecting light.
d) They appear when it snows in the North Pole.

4. What is the meaning of 'particles' as used in the passage?
a) Animals
b) Plants
c) Small pieces or bits
d) Large objects

5. If the passage included a map, what would it most likely show?
a) Locations where the Northern Lights can be seen.
b) Different countries in the world.
c) The sun and its particles.
d) Animals found near the North Pole.

create inspire teach

			✓ checklist
PROMPT: Where and how does the Aurora Borealis happen?			
Restate the question			
Answer the question			
Cite evidence from the text	• The author states.. • In the passage, it mentioned that... • From the reading, I learned...		
Explain how the evidence proves your answer	• This demonstrates that • From this, we can understand that • This detail shed light on		
Summarize	• In a nutshell, • After reading, I know... • The main thing to remember		
CAPITAL LETTER, PUNCTUATION MARKS, CORRECT SPELLING			

create inspire teach

SPRING ANSWER KEYS

Name: **ANSWER KEY**

WALLY'S WACKY WEATHER MACHINE

Wally was not your average eight-year-old. While most kids his age played with toy cars, Wally loved to tinker with gadgets and gizmos. His room was filled with bits and bobs of old machines and weird inventions. One rainy spring morning, Wally decided to create something extraordinary - a Weather Machine!

After hours of twisting wires, tightening bolts, and attaching what seemed like a hundred buttons, Wally's Weather Machine was ready. He had dreamed of making sunny days for picnics and gentle breezes for kite flying. But when he pressed the big red button, something went hilariously wrong.

Instead of a sunny spring day, snowflakes began to fall from the sky! Wally watched in astonishment as his backyard turned into a winter wonderland. He giggled and ran outside to build a snowman in the middle of spring.

The next day, Wally tried to fix the machine. This time, autumn leaves started swirling around as soon as he turned it on. Leaves of orange, red, and yellow danced in the air, and Wally found himself in a pile of leaves, laughing.

Each day brought a new surprise. One morning, flowers bloomed instantly in his garden, bees buzzing happily. Another day, a gust of wind carried away his hat, and he chased it around like a playful puppy.

Wally's neighbors were puzzled by the strange weather but found joy in the unexpected. They had snowball fights and then the next day they went leaf-jumping. Mrs. Garcia, next door, even started wearing her sunhat and winter scarf at the same time!

Finally, Wally managed to set things right, and the weather returned to normal. But the town agreed that Wally's Wacky Weather Machine had made this the most unforgettable spring ever. Wally learned that sometimes, the best inventions create not just things but wonderful memories.

1. <u>Part A:</u> What was Wally's goal in creating the Weather Machine?

A. To cause trouble in his neighborhood

B. To make every day snowy for building snowmen

C. To enjoy different seasons in one day

<u>D. To create perfect weather for outdoor activities</u>

<u>Part B:</u> Which piece of text supports your answer to Part A?

A. "Wally loved to tinker with gadgets and gizmos."

<u>B. "He had dreamed of making sunny days for picnics and gentle breezes for kite flying."</u>

C. "Snowflakes began to fall from the sky!"

D. "The next day, Wally tried to fix the machine."

2. What does the phrase 'turned into a winter wonderland' suggest about the weather?

A. It became very hot and sunny.

B. It started raining heavily.

<u>C. It snowed in spring.</u>

D. Flowers bloomed everywhere.

3. Which of the following happened because of Wally's Weather Machine?

A. Snow in spring

B. Autumn leaves swirling

C. Flowers blooming instantly

<u>D. All of the above</u>

4. Find an antonym for the word 'ordinary?'

A. Average

B. Normal

<u>C. Unique</u>

D. Similar

create inspire teach

				✓ checklist
PROMPT:	How did Wally's weather machine help to create wonderful memories for the town?			
Restate the question	Wally's weather machine helped to create wonderful memories for the town		**ANSWER KEY**	✓
Answer the question	because the people in the town were able to have snowball fights, and then the next day, they went leaf-jumping.			✓
Cite evidence from the text	• According to the text, • The text says, • It is shown in the text,	According to the text, the town agreed that Wally's Wacky Weather Machine had made this the most unforgettable spring ever.		✓
Explain how the evidence proves your answer	• When I read__, I felt… • This part seems important because, • This part shows…	This part shows the town found joy in the unexpected weather and made the most of it!		✓
Summarize	• Piecing everything together… • Drawing everything together… • The big lesson is…	The big lesson is sometimes, the best inventions create not just things but wonderful memories.		✓
	CAPITAL LETTER, PUNCTUATION MARKS, CORRECT SPELLING			✓

Wally's weather machine helped to create wonderful memories for the town because the people in the town were able to have snowball fights, and then the next day, they went leaf-jumping. According to the text, the town agreed that Wally's Wacky Weather Machine had made this the most unforgettable spring ever. This part shows the town found joy in the unexpected weather and made the most of it! The big lesson is sometimes, the best inventions create not just things but wonderful memories.

create inspire teach

Name: _____ ANSWER KEY

LUNA AND THE LOST BIRD

One sunny spring morning, Luna found a tiny bird on the ground. The baby bird, with its fluffy feathers, chirped softly. It had fallen from its nest during a storm last night. Luna knew she had to help. She gently picked up the bird and placed it in a cozy shoebox. "Don't worry, little one. I'll find your home," Luna whispered.

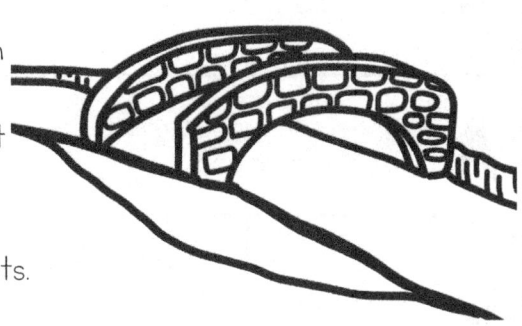

Luna and her mom searched the garden for the nest. Along the way, Luna learned that different birds build different types of nests. Robins use mud and grass, while sparrows like to use sticks and feathers..

They finally found the nest high in an oak tree, but it was too high for Luna to reach. Luna had an idea! She called Mr. Jenkins, their neighbor, who was a firefighter. He came with a tall ladder and carefully placed the baby bird back in its nest.

The mother bird returned, chirping happily. Luna felt a warm glow in her heart as she watched the bird family reunite.

That evening, Luna drew a picture of the birds and their nest. She went to bed dreaming of the little bird and the big adventure they had shared on this beautiful spring day.

1. Why did Luna decide to help the baby bird?
A. It was chirping loudly.
<u>B. It had fallen from its nest.</u>
C. It was flying too low.
D. It was lost in her garden.

2. What is the theme of the story?
A. Birds should be left alone.
<u>B. Helping others is rewarding.</u>
C. Storms are dangerous for birds.
D. Neighbors are always firefighters.

3. How did Luna feel after reuniting the baby bird with its family?
A. Confused
B. Scared
<u>C. Happy.</u>
D. Angry

4. What does the phrase "a warm glow in her heart" mean in the context of the story?
A. Luna was feeling hot.
<u>B. Luna was feeling proud and happy.</u>
C. Luna had a light in her heart.
D. Luna was feeling ill.

5. What is a synonym for "reunite" as used in the story?
A. Separate
<u>B. Join again</u>
C. Confuse
D. Leave

create inspire teach

PROMPT: What lesson did Luna learn from helping the baby bird? ✓ checklist

Restate the question	When Lunda helped the baby bird she learned that	**ANSWER KEY**	✓
Answer the question	helping other can be really rewarding.		✓
Cite evidence from the text	• One important moment from the story… • An example from the text is… • As stated in the text,	An example from the text is when the author said that Luna felt a warm glow in her heart as she watched the bird family reunite.	✓
Explain how the evidence proves your answer	• This evidence shows me, • This proves, • As you can see,	This proves Luna felt proud and happy about helping the baby bird.	✓
Summarize	• The text leaves us thinking about… • One thing is certain after reading… • Reflecting on the story…	One thing is certain after reading, Luna loved helping the baby bird and I am sure she will help other animals and people in the future.	✓
	CAPITAL LETTER, PUNCTUATION MARKS, CORRECT SPELLING		✓

When Lunda helped the baby bird she learned that helping other can be really rewarding. An example from the text is when the author said that Luna felt a warm glow in her heart as she watched the bird family reunite. This proves Luna felt proud and happy about helping the baby bird. One thing is certain after reading, Luna loved helping the baby bird, and I am sure she will help other animals and people in the future.

create inspire teach

Name: _____ **ANSWER KEY**

PABLO'S PAINTBRUSH

In a very gray town, a boy named Pablo found a special paintbrush. This wasn't just any paintbrush; it was magical! With it, Pablo could paint pictures that came to life. He decided to make his boring town beautiful by painting bright and happy spring scenes on the walls.

But even with all the new colors, Pablo noticed that people were too busy to look at his paintings. This made him sad, and he wondered if his magic paintings really mattered.

Then, one day, an elderly lady saw him feeling down and said, "Your paintings are lovely, but people need to find joy themselves." Pablo thought hard about her words. He realized he might not be able to make people notice the beauty around them, but he could teach them how to create it themselves.

So, Pablo started to teach the townspeople how to paint. At first, only a few people were interested, but soon more and more joined in. As they painted together, they began to smile more and see the beauty in everyday things, not just in Pablo's magical paintings.

Pablo learned that the real magic wasn't just in his paintbrush. The best magic happened when he shared his love for painting with others and helped them find happiness in making something beautiful.

The town wasn't gray anymore; it was full of colors and joy because Pablo helped everyone see the world in a new way.

1. Part A: What did Pablo find that changed the town?

A. A book of spells

<u>B. A magical paintbrush</u>

C. A hidden treasure

D. A map of the town

Part B: Which part of the text supports your answer to Part A?

<u>A. "Pablo found a magical paintbrush that made his drawings come to life."</u>

B. "He started painting vibrant spring scenes on the town's walls."

C. "But Pablo noticed that people were too busy to admire his art."

D. "Pablo learned that the true magic wasn't just in his paintbrush."

2. Part A: What lesson did Pablo learn from the elderly lady?

A. That art is not important

B. That he needed a new paintbrush

<u>C. That real change must come from within people</u>

D. That people don't like colorful walls

Part B: How did Pablo apply this lesson?

A. By leaving the town

<u>B. By teaching the townsfolk to paint</u>

C. By painting over his murals

D. By finding another magical object

4. What does 'disheartened' mean as used in the text?

A. Excited

B. Confused

<u>C. Sad and losing hope</u>

D. Energized

create inspire teach

PROMPT: How does Pablo's understanding of joy and beauty change throughout the story? ✓ checklist

Restate the question		Pablos understanding of joy and beauty changed throughout the story	**ANSWER KEY**	✓
Answer the question		because at the beginning he thought the townsfolk would simply enjoy the art work, but he realized that that couldn't appreciate it until they found the joy in themselves.		✓
Cite evidence from the text	• (The character) says… • To support this idea, in paragraph ___, it says • A key detail from the text is…	The elderly lady says, "Your paintings are lovely, but people need to find joy themselves."		✓
Explain how the evidence proves your answer	• I noticed… • Because of this, I think… • An interesting part is when…	Because of this, Pablo started to teach the people in the town how to paint.		✓
Summarize	• In the end, it's clear that… • Looking back, • It all comes down to…	In the end, the town wasn't gray anymore; it was full of colors and joy because Pablo helped everyone see the world in a new way.		✓
	CAPITAL LETTER, PUNCTUATION MARKS, CORRECT SPELLING			✓

Pablos understanding of joy and beauty changed throughout the story because at the beginning he thought the townsfolk would simply enjoy the art work, but he realized that that couldn't appreciate it until they found the joy in themselves. The elderly lady says, "Your paintings are lovely, but people need to find joy themselves." Because of this, Pablo started to teach the people in the town how to paint. In the end, the town wasn't gray anymore; it was full of colors and joy because Pablo helped everyone see the world in a new way.

create inspire teach

Name: _____ ANSWER KEY

THE ADVENTURES OF CAPTAIN BLOOM

Captain Bloom, a kind-hearted pirate, steered his ship through the waves. He and his crew were on an adventure to find a magical island that only appeared every hundred years during the spring season. This island was hidden, but he heard it had the most wonderful plants and animals.

Captain Bloom had an old map that showed the way to the island. "This will be our greatest adventure!" he told his crew.

As they sailed, they entered a thick fog. Not disheartened by the fog, he kept going. When the fog cleared, the beautiful island appeared. The island was full of rainbow-colored trees, shiny birds, and singing flowers.

Captain Bloom wanted to take some of these magical things back with him. "We'll be the richest pirates ever!" he thought.

As he tried to take a sparkling rock, the island began to shake. Captain Bloom realized he was wrong. "This island is not for taking but for learning and enjoying," he said to his crew.

They decided to leave the island as it was, taking only their memories and stories of their adventure. Captain Bloom learned that some treasures are meant to be admired, not taken.

When they sailed away, the island vanished, but the lesson Captain Bloom learned stayed with him forever.

1. Part A: Why did Captain Bloom and his crew go on an adventure?
A. To escape from enemies
B. To find a magical island
C. To hide their treasure
D. To visit friends

Part B: Which part of the text supports your answer to Part A?
A. "Captain Bloom, a kind-hearted pirate, steered his ship through the waves."
B. "This island was hidden, but he heard it had the most wonderful plants and animals."
C. "Captain Bloom wanted to take some of these magical things back with him."
D. "They decided to leave the island as it was, taking only their memories and stories."

2. What lesson did Captain Bloom learn from his adventure?
A. Magical islands appear every day.
B. Fog is dangerous for ships.
C. Treasures are meant to be taken and sold.
D. Some treasures should be admired, not taken.

3. How do Captain Bloom's actions on the island contribute to the story's message?
A. His decision to take treasures shows the value of wealth.
B. His realization and decision to leave the treasures behind showed his learning and respect for nature.
C. His ability to steer the ship demonstrates his skill as a captain.
D. His interaction with the crew shows how to lead a team.

4. What does the word 'vanished' mean in the context of the story?
A. Appeared suddenly
B. Changed color
C. Disappeared from sight
D. Became larger

create inspire teach

PROMPT: What lesson did Captain Bloom learn on the island?

✓ checklist

ANSWER KEY

Restate the question	The lesson Captain Bloom learned on the island		✓
Answer the question	was that some treasures were to be admired, not taken.		✓
Cite evidence from the text	• In the beginning/middle/end of the story, it mentions... • The narrator point out... • Drawing from the text...	Drawing from the text, Captain Bloom said that as he tried to take a sparkling rock, the island began to shake. he realized he was wrong. "This island is not for taking but for learning and enjoying."	✓
Explain how the evidence proves your answer	• This conversation shows... • What the characters did here tells us that... • From what I read, I know this is important because	What the character did here is learn an important lesson about respecting nature.	✓
Summarize	• After reading the text, I realized... • Overall, the story teaches us... • All in all,	All in all, Captain Bloom learned that nature should be respected and not taken.	✓
	CAPITAL LETTER, PUNCTUATION MARKS, CORRECT SPELLING		✓

The lesson Captain Bloom learned on the island was that some treasures were to be admired, not taken. Drawing from the text, Captain Bloom said that as he tried to take a sparkling rock, the island began to shake. He realized he was wrong. "This island is not for taking but for learning and enjoying." What the character did here is to learn an important lesson about respecting nature. All in all, Captain Bloom learned that nature should be respected and not taken.

create inspire teach

Name: _____ **ANSWER KEY**

THE PICNIC AT THE END OF THE RAINBOW

On a beautiful spring morning, a rainbow stretched across the sky above Greenwood. Mia, Jack, Lily, Omar, and Emily, a group of curious friends, were thrilled. "Let's find where the rainbow ends!" suggested Mia.

As they embarked on their journey, Jack, who was always in a rush, complained, "We need to hurry, or we'll never get there!" He was so focused on the destination that he almost missed the beauty around him.

While walking through lush green meadows, they saw butterflies fluttering and flowers blooming. Fascinated, Omar said, "Rainbows and butterflies both need sunlight. They remind us of nature's magic." Near a stream, Lily admired the wildflowers. "These flowers are like nature's paintbrush," she mused.

When they reached a hill where the rainbow seemed to descend, Jack realized something important. There was no pot of gold, but the scenery was beautiful. He learned that the journey and the time spent with friends were more valuable than any treasure.

The friends laid out their picnic blankets, enjoying snacks in the sun. Jack shared his newfound insight, "I've learned that sometimes, slowing down lets us appreciate the real treasures in life."

Their adventure wasn't just about finding the rainbow's end; it was about discovering the joy in every step of their journey together.

1. <u>Part A</u>: What does Mia propose at the beginning of the story?
A. To have a picnic
<u>B. To find the end of the rainbow</u>
C. To go back home
D. To play a game

<u>Part B</u>: Where in the text does it show Mia's proposal?
A. "Mia, Jack, Lily, Omar, and Emily were thrilled."
<u>B. "Let's find where the rainbow ends!" suggested Mia.</u>
C. "Jack, who was always in a rush, complained."
D. "They saw butterflies fluttering and flowers blooming."

2. <u>Part A</u>: What lesson does Jack learn?
A. Rainbows always lead to gold.
B. Adventures are a waste of time.
<u>C. The journey and friendships are valuable.</u>
D. Butterflies are essential for rainbows.

<u>Part B</u>: Which part of the text supports Jack's lesson?
A. "Jack realized something important."
<u>B. "He learned that the journey and the time spent with friends were more valuable than any treasure."</u>
C. "Omar, fascinated, explained."
D. "Lily admired the wildflowers."

4. What does the word 'curious' mean as used to describe Mia, Jack, Lily, Omar, and Emily?
A. Scared of new experiences
B. Uninterested in exploring
<u>C. Eager to learn or explore new things</u>
D. Confused by the rainbow

PROMPT: What lesson did Jack learn on their journey to find the rainbow?

✓ checklist

Restate the question	The lesson Jack learned on their journey to find the rainbow	**ANSWER KEY**	✓
Answer the question		was that sometimes, slowing down lets us appreciate the real treasures in life	✓
Cite evidence from the text	• A quote that shows this. • From the dialogue, it's clear that... • The author mentions...	A quote that show this is "There was no pot of gold, but the scenery was beautiful. He learned that the journey and the time spent with friends were more valuable than any treasure."	✓
Explain how the evidence proves your answer	• This made me think of when... • It's interesting that the story says... • This part seems important because...	This part is important because it shows that Jack learned that it isn't about the destination, but about the journey.	✓
Summarize	• To sum it all up, • In conclusion, • Without a doubt,	To sum it all up, Jack learned about the importance of slowing down and enjoying the things and people around him.	✓
	CAPITAL LETTER, PUNCTUATION MARKS, CORRECT SPELLING		✓

The lesson Jack learned on their journey to find the rainbow was that sometimes, slowing down lets us appreciate the real treasures in life. A quote that show this is "There was no pot of gold, but the scenery was beautiful. He learned that the journey and the time spent with friends were more valuable than any treasure." This part is important because it shows that Jack learned that it isn't about the destination but about the journey. To sum it all up, Jack learned about the importance of slowing down and enjoying the things and people around him.

create inspire teach

Name: _____ ANSWER KEY

SPRING FESTIVALS AROUND THE WORLD

Spring is a magical season that brings warmth, blooms, and celebrations across the globe. Each corner of the world welcomes spring in its own way. Let's explore some of the ways spring is celebrated around the world!

Holi in India

In India, spring bursts into color with the festival of Holi, also known as the Festival of Colors. It's a joyous day when people forget their worries and splash bright colors on each other. Holi symbolizes new beginnings, the victory of good over evil, and is a time for laughter, dance, and sweet treats.

Cherry Blossom Festivals in Japan

In Japan, the Cherry Blossom Festival, or "Hanami," celebrates the fleeting beauty of cherry blossoms. Families and friends gather under the pink and white blossoms for picnics and songs, embracing the <u>transient</u> beauty of life. The cherry blossoms remind us to appreciate every moment.

Easter Traditions

Around the world, Easter welcomes spring with symbols of new life, like eggs and bunnies. People decorate Easter eggs, join in egg hunts, and gather for festive meals. Easter traditions vary, but the spirit of joy and renewal is universal.

The Spirit of Spring

These spring festivals, from Holi to Easter, share a common thread—they celebrate life, renewal, and the beauty of nature. They remind us to cherish the moment, embrace change, and look forward to new beginnings. As spring unfolds, let's carry the spirit of these festivals in our hearts, welcoming the season of growth and happiness.

1. What is the main idea of the passage?
A. Spring is a season of cold and snow.
<u>B. Spring festivals around the world celebrate life, renewal, and the beauty of nature.</u>
C. Easter is celebrated in the same way around the world.
D. Cherry blossoms last all year round.

2. How do Holi and Easter traditions reflect the spirit of spring?
A. By encouraging people to stay indoors
<u>B. Through celebrations that embrace life and new beginnings</u>
C. By marking the end of outdoor activities
D. Through quiet reflection and solitude

3. What does the word 'transient' mean in the context of cherry blossoms?
<u>A. Lasting a short time</u>
B. Happening at night
C. Blooming
D. Brightly colored

4. What effect does spring have on people around the world?
A. It causes people to stay indoors.
<u>B. It causes people to celebrate life and new beginnings.</u>
C. It causes all festivals to occur in India.
D. It causes outdoor activities to be canceled.

create inspire teach

PROMPT: What are some ways spring is celebrated around the world?			✓ checklist
Restate the question	Spring is celebrated in many way around the world.	**ANSWER KEY**	✓
Answer the question	In India, they celebrate Holi; in Japan, they celebrate the cherry blossom festival; and Easter is celebrated in many countries around the world.		✓
Cite evidence from the text	• According to the text, • The author points out... • This article states that	According to the text, these festivals help to welcome spring in different ways.	✓
Explain how the evidence proves your answer	• This means that... • So, what they are saying • In other words,	This means that even these spring festivals, from Holi to Easter, share a common thread—they celebrate life, renewal, and the beauty of nature.	✓
Summarize	• After thinking about all this • When we put all the pieces together, • In short,	In short, these festivals help us to remember to cherish the moment, embrace change, and look forward to new beginnings.	✓
	CAPITAL LETTER, PUNCTUATION MARKS, CORRECT SPELLING		✓

Spring is celebrated in many way around the world. In India, they celebrate Holi; in Japan, they celebrate the cherry blossom festival; and Easter is celebrated in many countries around the world. According to the text, these festivals help to welcome spring in different ways. This means that even these spring festivals, from Holi to Easter, share a common thread—they celebrate life, renewal, and the beauty of nature. In short, these festivals help us to remember to cherish the moment, embrace change, and look forward to new beginnings.

create inspire teach

Name: _____ ANSWER KEY

SPRING STARS AND CONSTELLATIONS: A NIGHT SKY ADVENTURE

As the days grow longer and the nights get warmer, spring invites us to explore the twinkling stars and <u>constellations</u> that light up the night sky. Let's take a look at the starry nights of spring!

One of the most famous spring constellations is Leo, the Lion. If you look up at the sky on a clear spring night, you can find Leo by looking for a group of stars that form a shape like a crouching lion. According to ancient myths, Leo was a fierce lion that lived in the sky. The brightest star in Leo is called Regulus, which means "little king," shining brightly as the lion's heart.

Another constellation is Virgo, the Maiden, or a lady. Virgo is easier to spot if you find Spica, its brightest star. It looks like a sparkling diamond. People long ago imagined Virgo as a kind and gentle maiden holding a spike of wheat, which is why Spica shines so brightly.

Lastly, don't miss Boötes, the Herdsman, which looks like a kite in the sky. The brightest star in Boötes is Arcturus. The story goes that Boötes watches over the bears, Big Bear and Little Bear, which circle the North Star.

These constellations are not just groups of stars; they tell stories that have been passed down from generation to generation. As you gaze at the night sky this spring, imagine the ancient tales and adventures that these stars have inspired. Maybe you'll even come up with your own stories!

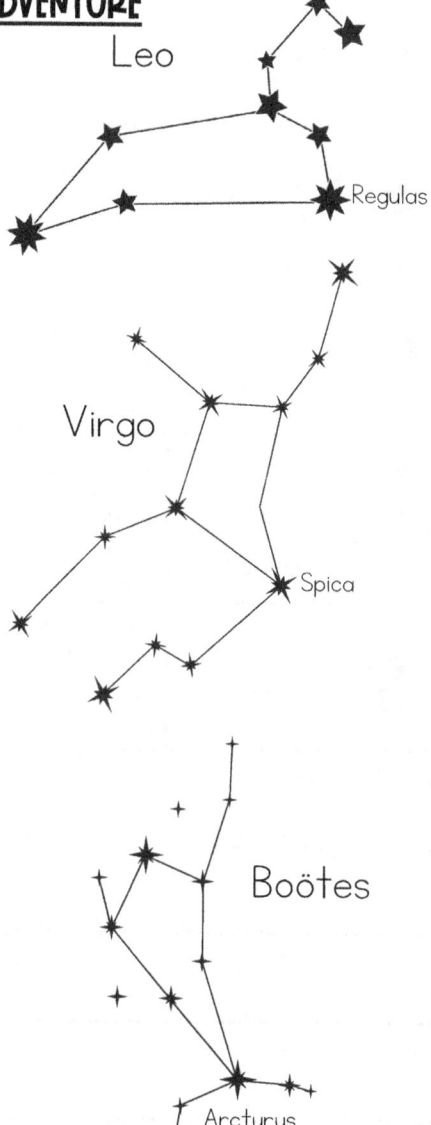

1. What purpose do the stories behind constellations serve according to the passage?
A. To make the sky look more interesting
B. To guide sailors at sea
<u>C. To inspire imagination and share ancient tales</u>
D. To help people predict the weather

2. How are the constellations Leo and Virgo different?
A. Leo represents a kind and gentle figure, while Virgo symbolizes strength.
<u>B. Leo symbolizes a fierce lion, while Virgo is imagined as a kind and gentle maiden.</u>
C. Both represent animals in the sky.
D. Both are related to agricultural symbols.

3. What does the word 'constellations' mean as used in the text?
<u>A. A group of stars forming a recognizable pattern</u>
B. A single bright star in the night sky
C. A mythological creature
D. A type of telescope

4. Which statement is an opinion?
A. The constellation Leo looks like a crouching lion.
B. Spica is the brightest star in Virgo.
<u>C. The stories of constellations inspire imagination.</u>
D. Arcturus is one of the brightest stars visible.

create inspire teach

			✓ checklist
PROMPT:	How did many generations use story telling to understand what the constellations looked like?		
Restate the question		Many generations used story telling to understand what the constellations looked like **ANSWER KEY**	✓
Answer the question		by describing how the stars went together to form figures in the sky, and then they came up with stories around those constellations.	✓
Cite evidence from the text	• Evidence from the article shows… • The author argues that… • Based on the text…	Based on the text, we can see that the constellation Leo is shaped like a lion, and the constellation Virgo is shaped like a lady.	✓
Explain how the evidence proves your answer	• That's interesting because it shows that… • This is important because… • The reason for this is …	This is important because it shows how people were looking for patterns in the sky.	✓
Summarize	• To conclude, • This all means that, • So, the big idea is	To conclude, many generations used storytelling to understand what the constellations looked like.	✓
	CAPITAL LETTER, PUNCTUATION MARKS, CORRECT SPELLING		✓

Many generations used story telling to understand what the constellations looked like by describing how the stars went together to form figures in the sky, and then they came up with stories around those constellations. Based on the text, we can see that the constellation Leo is shaped like a lion, and the constellation Virgo is shaped like a lady. This is important because it shows how people were looking for patterns in the sky. To conclude, many generations used storytelling to understand what the constellations looked like.

create inspire teach

Name: _____ ANSWER KEY

THE BUSY BUILDERS OF SPRING: BIRDS AND THEIR NESTS

When spring arrives, it brings a flurry of activity in the trees and bushes. All kinds of birds become busy builders, creating nests for their families. Have you ever wondered how these feathered friends make their homes and care for their babies? Let's find out!

Birds build nests to keep their eggs and baby birds safe and warm. Each bird species has its own special way of making a nest. Some birds, like robins, use mud and grass to make a cup-shaped home in the branches of trees. Others, like sparrows, might use sticks, feathers, and even bits of paper to create a <u>snug</u> nest in a bush or on a building.

Materials aren't the only thing that varies; so does location. Eagles, for example, build giant nests high up in tall trees or on cliffs. They use sticks and branches, and their nests can be big enough for a person to sit in!

But why do birds go through all this trouble in spring? Spring is the perfect time for birds to lay eggs and raise their young. The warmer weather means there are plenty of insects and worms to feed hungry baby birds. By the time the babies are ready to leave the nest, the world is full of food, and the temperature is warm.

Caring for their young is a big job. Birds keep their eggs warm by sitting on them until they hatch. Once the baby birds arrive, parents work tirelessly to feed them, sometimes bringing food back to the nest hundreds of times a day!

The nest is made from twigs, leaves, and grass, carefully woven together. Birds choose safe places to build their nests to protect the eggs from predators.

Chicks grow inside the egg until they are big enough to break through the shell. When they first hatch, they rely on their parents to bring them food and keep them warm. In a few weeks, these chicks will grow feathers and learn to fly.

1. <u>Part A</u>: Why do birds build nests in the spring?
A. To prepare for winter
B. To attract a mate
<u>C. To keep their eggs and baby birds safe and warm</u>
D. To find food more easily

<u>Part B</u>: Which detail from the text supports your answer to Part A?
<u>A. "Birds build nests to keep their eggs and baby birds safe and warm."</u>
B. "Eagles, for example, build giant nests high up in tall trees or on cliffs."
C. "Spring is the perfect time for birds to lay their eggs and raise their young."
D. "Birds keep their eggs warm by sitting on them until they hatch."

3. How do the nesting materials of robins and sparrows differ?
A. Robins use sticks and feathers; sparrows use mud and grass.
B. Robins and sparrows both use mud and grass exclusively.
<u>C. Robins use mud and grass; sparrows use sticks, feathers, and bits of paper.</u>
D. There is no difference; all birds use the same materials.

4. What does 'snug' mean as used in the text?
A. Loose and uncomfortable
B. Cold and unwelcoming
<u>C. Cozy and secure</u>
D. Large and open

create inspire teach

PROMPT: Why do birds build their nests in the spring?

✓ checklist

Restate the question	Birds build their nests in the spring	**ANSWER KEY**	✓
Answer the question	because its is the perfect time for birds to lay eggs and raise their young.		✓
Cite evidence from the text	• The author shows that… • A quote that stands out is… • As evidence, the passage says…	As evidence from the passage, the warmer weather means there are plenty of insects and worms to feed hungry baby birds.	✓
Explain how the evidence proves your answer	• What this tells us is … • So, if you think about it,… • This helps us understand that …	This helps me understand why birds build their nests in the spring.	✓
Summarize	• From what we've learned, • Putting it all together, • In the end, we can say that	From what we've learned Birds build their nests in the spring because its is the perfect time for birds to lay eggs and raise their young.	✓
	CAPITAL LETTER, PUNCTUATION MARKS, CORRECT SPELLING		✓

Birds build their nests in the spring because its is the perfect time for birds to lay eggs and raise their young. As evidence from the passage, the warmer weather means there are plenty of insects and worms to feed hungry baby birds. This helps me understand why birds build their nests in the spring. From what we've learned Birds build their nests in the spring because its is the perfect time for birds to lay eggs and raise their young.

create inspire teach

Name: _____ ANSWER KEY

THE SCIENCE BEHIND SPRING BLOOMS

Have you ever wondered why so many flowers start to bloom when spring rolls around? After a long, cold winter, the world suddenly bursts into color with all sorts of flowers. Let's dive into the science that wakes up the flowers every spring!

When spring comes, the days get longer, and the sun shines more. This extra sunlight is like a wake-up call for sleeping flowers. The warm rays tell the flowers that it's time to grow. Sunlight is super important because it helps plants make their food through a process called <u>photosynthesis</u>. This is how flowers get the energy to bloom into the beautiful colors we see.

Temperature plays a big role too. Many flowers need the warmth of spring to start growing. During winter, they rest underground as bulbs or seeds, waiting for the right moment. When the air and soil warm up, it signals to the flowers that the conditions are just right for them to come out and bloom.

Soil nutrients are the food for flowers. Just like we need vitamins to grow strong and healthy, flowers need nutrients from the soil. In spring, the rain helps mix these nutrients up, making it easier for the roots of plants to soak them up. This meal of nutrients gives flowers everything they need to bloom brightly.

All these factors work together to create the beautiful spring scenery we love. Sunlight, warmth, and nutrients are nature's way of painting the world with flowers. So, the next time you see a field of blooming flowers, you'll know it's all thanks to the science of spring!

<u>Glossary:</u>
Photosynthesis: The process by which plants turn sunlight into food

1. <u>Part A:</u> What makes flowers start to bloom in spring?
A. More rainfall
<u>B. Longer days and more sunlight</u>
C. Animals coming out of hibernation
D. People planting more flowers

<u>Part B:</u> Which detail from the text supports your answer to Part A?
<u>A. "The warm rays tell the flowers that it's time to grow."</u>
B. "During winter, they rest underground as bulbs or seeds."
C. "Soil nutrients are the food for flowers."
D. "Sunlight is super important because it helps plants make their food."

3. What does 'photosynthesis' mean as used in the text?
A. The process by which plants lose their leaves
B. The process by which plants absorb water
<u>C. The process by which plants turn sunlight into food</u>
D. The process by which plants sleep during winter

4. Which statement is a fact?
A. Spring is the most beautiful season.
B. All flowers bloom at the same time in spring.
<u>C. Flowers need sunlight to perform photosynthesis.</u>
D. Without rain, flowers would still bloom just as brightly.

5.
Cause	Effect
The weather gets warmer	→

A. It causes flowers to remain dormant.
<u>B. It signals flowers to start growing.</u>
C. It makes flowers require less sunlight.
D. It decreases the nutrients in the soil.

create inspire teach

			✓ checklist
PROMPT:	Why do flowers bloom in the spring?		
Restate the question		Flowers boom in the spring **ANSWER KEY**	✓
Answer the question		because the extra sunlight is like a wake-up call for sleeping flowers.	✓
Cite evidence from the text	• Highlighting this point, the text states… • From the text we can see… • Supporting this idea, the text describes…	Highlighting this point, the text states Sunlight is super important because it helps plants make their food through a process called photosynthesis.	✓
Explain how the evidence proves your answer	• Because of this, we can see that… • This makes me think that… • It's like when…	Because of this we can see that many flowers need the warmth of spring to start growing.	✓
Summarize	• To wrap this up, • The main thing to remember is. • After looking at everything, I think	To wrap it up, flowers bloom in the spring because of the extra sunlight.	✓
	CAPITAL LETTER, PUNCTUATION MARKS, CORRECT SPELLING		✓

Flowers boom in the spring because the extra sunlight is like a wake-up call for sleeping flowers. Highlighting this point, the text states sunlight is super important because it helps plants make their food through a process called photosynthesis. Because of this we can see that many flowers need the warmth of spring to start growing. To wrap it up, flowers bloom in the spring because of the extra sunlight.

create inspire teach

Name: _____ ANSWER KEY

SPRING'S UNDERGROUND HEROES

When spring comes, not all the magic happens above ground; there's a busy world underground too! Let's take a peek at what goes on beneath the soil and how it helps everything above it bloom.

As the weather warms up, the soil becomes alive with worms, insects, and tiny creatures too small to see. These underground residents are super important for making the soil healthy and ready for plants to grow.

Worms play a big role in spring. They move through the soil, making tiny tunnels that let air and water get to plant roots. They also eat dead leaves, turning them into food for plants. This is a bit like making a vitamin-rich meal for the garden!

Insects are busy too. They help by spreading pollen from flower to flower and keeping harmful bugs away from plants. Each bug has its own special job that keeps the garden healthy.

Healthy soil is like a cozy bed for plants. It holds onto water and gives plants the nutrients they need to grow strong. It also supports the plants, helping them reach up towards the sunlight.

So, next time you see flowers blooming or trees budding in spring, remember there's a whole team of underground heroes helping them grow. Worms, insects, and all the tiny life in the soil work together to create the beautiful spring scenery we all enjoy.

1. Part A: What role do worms play in helping plants grow?
A. They pollinate the flowers.
B. They make tunnels in the soil for air and water.
C. They block sunlight from reaching the plants.
D. They scare away the insects.

Part B: Which detail from the text supports your answer to Part A?
A. "They also eat dead leaves, turning them into food for plants."
B. "Insects are busy too."
C. "Healthy soil is like a cozy bed for plants."
D. "Worms move through the soil, making tiny tunnels that let air and water get to plant roots."

2. How do worms and insects contribute differently to the health of the garden?
A. Worms make tunnels to let air and water into the soil, while insects spread pollen and protect plants from harmful bugs.
B. Worms and insects both eat dead leaves.
C. Worms pollinate flowers, and insects make tunnels.
D. Worms harm plants, and insects help plants grow.

3. Which statement is an opinion?
A. Worms eat dead leaves and turn them into plant food.
B. Insects spread pollen from flower to flower.
C. Healthy soil is crucial for plant growth.
D. Spring's underground heroes make the world a better place.

4. What do worms, insects, and tiny creatures in the soil all contribute to?
A. Making the soil dry
B. Preventing plants from growing
C. Enriching the soil, making it healthy for plants
D. All of the above

create inspire teach

			✓ checklist
PROMPT: How do worms, insects, and tiny creatures help to get the soil ready for plants?			
Restate the question		Worms, insects, and tiny creatures help the soil get ready for plants **ANSWER KEY**	✓
Answer the question		by making tunnels to let air and water into the soil, spreading pollen and protecting plants from harmful bugs.	✓
Cite evidence from the text	• As shown in the paragraph -- • Drawing evidence from the text, • When reading this article, I learned...	As shown in paragraph 3, worms move through the soil, making tiny tunnels that let air and water get to plant roots. They also eat dead leaves, turning them into food for plants.	✓
Explain how the evidence proves your answer	• The big idea here is ... • This example shows that • If we look closer, we can find out that ...	If we look closer we can find out that insects help by spreading pollen from flower to flower and keeping harmful bugs away from plants.	✓
Summarize	• All in all, it seems like • So, what we found out is ... • In summary,	All in all, it seems that worms, insects, and all the tiny life in the soil work together to create the beautiful spring scenery we all enjoy.	✓
CAPITAL LETTER, PUNCTUATION MARKS, CORRECT SPELLING			✓

Worms, insects, and tiny creatures help the soil get ready for plants by making tunnels to let air and water into the soil, spreading pollen and protecting plants from harmful bugs. As shown in paragraph 3, worms move through the soil, making tiny tunnels that let air and water get to plant roots. They also eat dead leaves, turning them into food for plants. If we look closer we can find out that insects help by spreading pollen from flower to flower and keeping harmful bugs away from plants. All in all, it seems that worms, insects, and all the tiny life in the soil work together to create the beautiful spring scenery we all enjoy.

create inspire teach

SUMMER ANSWER KEYS

Name: _____ ANSWER KEY

THE JOURNEY OF A RAINDROP: THE WATER CYCLE

Water is always moving. From the sky to the land and then back again, it travels in a cycle. This cycle is made up of a four steps: evaporation, condensation, precipitation, and collection. Let's follow the cycle to learn how a drop of water can travel around the world!

It all starts with the sun, which heats up water in rivers, lakes, and oceans. The heat turns the water into vapor or steam. This process is called evaporation. The water vapor rises into the air, invisible to our eyes, and begins its journey upward.

As the water vapor goes higher, it reaches cooler air in the sky. When it cools down, it changes back into tiny drops of liquid water. This is called condensation. These tiny water droplets come together to form clouds!

When the clouds get heavy with water, the water falls back to the ground. This is precipitation. Precipitation can come down as rain, snow, sleet, or hail. It depends on how cold it is. Rain and snow are the most common forms that we see.

After the water reaches the ground, it collects in bodies of water. Some of it soaks into the soil and goes underground. Some of it runs over the soil and collects in puddles, streams, rivers, and eventually makes its way back to the oceans. Then the water is ready to start the cycle all over again.

The water cycle is important because it provides us with freshwater. Without it, the water would stay in one place and could become hard to find in some areas. The water cycle also keeps our planet at just the right temperature and helps all plants and animals live and grow. So, the next time you see a cloud or feel raindrops falling from the sky, remember the water cycle. It is a journey that has been happening on Earth for billions of years, and every drop of water has a story to tell about the many places it has been.

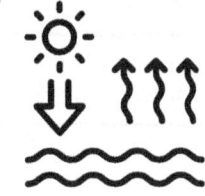

1. The passage states, "Water is always moving." Is this the author's opinion or a fact supported by the text?
A) It's the author's opinion.
B) It's a fact supported by the text.
C) It's a suggestion.
D) It's a prediction about the future.

2. What does the word "precipitation" mean in the context of the water cycle?
A) When water soaks into the ground
B) When water vapor turns into liquid and forms clouds
C) When water falls from clouds as rain, snow, sleet, or hail
D) When water moves from land back into oceans

3. What is the main idea of the passage about the water cycle?
A) The sun causes the water cycle to happen.
B) Water travels in a cycle which includes evaporation, condensation, precipitation, and collection.
C) Rain is the only form of precipitation.
D) Clouds are made of tiny water droplets.

4. Part A: What happens to water vapor when it cools down in the sky?
A) It turns into rain immediately.
B) It falls to the ground as precipitation.
C) It gathers into clouds.
D) It heats up and rises even higher.

Part B: Which piece of evidence from the text best supports the answer to Part A?
A) "The sun, which heats up water in rivers, lakes, and oceans."
B) "The water vapor rises into the air, invisible to our eyes, and begins its journey upward."
C) "When it cools down, it changes back into tiny drops of liquid water. These tiny droplets come together to form clouds."
D) "Precipitation can come down as rain, snow, sleet, or hail."

create inspire teach

			✓ checklist
PROMPT:	Why is the water cycle important?		
Restate the question	The water cycle is important	**ANSWER KEY**	✓
Answer the question	because without it, we would not have freshwater in some parts of Earth and the temperature wouldn't be right.		✓
Cite evidence from the text	• According to the text, • The text says, • It is shown in the text,	According to the text, without the water cycle, water would stay in one place and could become hard to find in some areas. The water cycle also keeps our planet at just the right temperature and helps all plants and animals live and grow.	✓
Explain how the evidence proves your answer	• This evidence shows me • This proves, • As you can see,	This proves how important the water cycle is for us on Earth.	✓
Summarize	• To sum it all up, • In conclusion, • Without a doubt,	Without a doubt, the water cycle help the plants, animals and people on Earth.	✓
	CAPITAL LETTER, PUNCTUATION MARKS, CORRECT SPELLING		✓

The water cycle is important because without it, we would not have freshwater in some parts of Earth and the temperature wouldn't be right. According to the text, without the water cycle, water would stay in one place and could become hard to find in some areas. The water cycle also keeps our planet at just the right temperature and helps all plants and animals live and grow. This proves how important the water cycle is for us on Earth. Without a doubt, the water cycle help the plants, animals and people on Earth.

create inspire teach

Name: _____ **ANSWER KEY**

WHY BEES ARE SO IMPORTANT

Bees might be small, but they have a big job in nature. Bees help plants grow, make honey, and keep forests and gardens healthy and beautiful.

When bees look for nectar in flowers, they get pollen all over their legs. As they move to the next flower, they take the pollen with them, which helps the flowers make seeds. This is called pollination. Lots of plants need pollination to make the fruits and vegetables we eat.

Bees also make honey from the nectar they collect from flowers. They take it back to their hive and work together to turn it into honey, which they eat when it's cold and there are no flowers around.

Bees are great helpers! They help trees and other plants to grow, which gives homes to birds and bugs. The plants also clean the air for us to breathe and give us food to eat. However, bees need our help. Bees can get sick from too many chemicals on plants or if they don't have enough flowers to visit. We can help bees by planting more flowers and taking care of the environment.

We should look after bees because they help so many plants and animals, including us! Without bees, we wouldn't have many of the foods we like to eat.

1. Part A How do bees help plants?

A) By giving them water

B) By making honey

C) By carrying pollen from one flower to another

D) By stinging them

Part B: What can happen if bees carry pollen to many flowers?

A) The flowers can turn into trees.

B) The flowers can change color.

C) More fruits and vegetables can grow.

D) The flowers can move to another place.

2. What is the main idea of the passage?

A) Bees make honey.

B) Bees are important to our environment.

C) Bees are small insects.

D) Bees live in hives.

3. The word "pollination" means...

A) Decoration of flowers

B) Protection of flowers

C) Growth of flowers

D) Transfer of pollen to help flowers make seeds

4. Which sentence is an opinion?

A) "Bees pollinate flowers, which helps plants grow."

B) "We should look after bees"

C) "Bees make honey from the nectar they collect from flowers."

D) "Bees can get sick from too many chemicals on plants."

create inspire teach

PROMPT: Why our bees important to our planet? ✓ checklist

Restate the question	Bees are important to our planet **ANSWER KEY**		✓
Answer the question	because they help help plants grow, make honey, and keep forests and gardens healthy and beautiful.		✓
Cite evidence from the text	• The author states… • In the passage, it mentioned that… • From the reading, I learned…	The author states that bees help to pollinate flowers which helps plants grow.	✓
Explain how the evidence proves your answer	• This demonstrates that • From this, we can understand that • This detail shed light on	This detail sheds light on how bees are important to our planet ebcause without plants, we would not have clean air or food to eat.	✓
Summarize	• In a nutshell, • After reading, I know… • The main thing to remember	In a nutshell. bees are so important for us and for our planet.	✓
	CAPITAL LETTER, PUNCTUATION MARKS, CORRECT SPELLING		✓

Bees are important to our planet because they help help plants grow, make honey, and keep forests and gardens healthy and beautiful. The author states that bees help to pollinate flowers which helps plants grow. This detail sheds light on how bees are important to our planet ebcause without plants, we would not have clean air or food to eat. In a nutshell. bees are so important for us and for our planet.

create inspire teach

Name: _____ ANSWER KEY

RECYCLING MATTERS!

Recycling is a process where we take things that we've used before, like paper, plastic, glass, and metal, and make them into new products. It starts when we put these materials into different bins at our homes or schools. Trucks take them to a recycling center where they are sorted, cleaned, and transformed.

Recycling matters a lot for our planet. When we recycle, we use less new material. This means we don't have to cut down as many trees for paper or use as much oil for making plastic. It also helps to save energy. Making products from recycled materials uses less energy than making them from new materials.

Another reason recycling is important is that it reduces the amount of waste sent to landfills. Landfills are where our trash goes when it can't be used again, and they can be harmful to the earth. They take up space and can pollute the air and water.

Recycling also helps to reduce greenhouse gas emissions, which are gases that make the Earth's atmosphere warmer. When we use less energy, we produce fewer of these gases. So recycling helps fight climate change.

By recycling, everyone can help protect the environment. It's a simple action that has a big impact on our planet's health.

   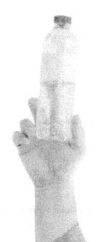   

1. Part A: What is the first step in the recycling process?
A) Cutting down trees
B) Sorting materials at the recycling center
<u>C) Putting used materials into different bins</u>
D) Transforming materials into new products

Part B: Which detail from the passage supports the answer to Part A?
A) "Recycling matters a lot for our planet."
B) "Trucks take them to a recycling center where they are sorted, cleaned, and transformed."
C) "Making products from recycled materials uses less energy."
<u>D) "It starts when we put these materials into different bins at our homes or schools."</u>

2. Part A: Why does recycling matter?
A) It makes trash collection easier.
B) It allows people to buy more products.
<u>C) It helps to save energy and reduce pollution.</u>
D) It creates more space for landfills.

Part B: Which two pieces of evidence from the text best support your answer to Part A? (Choose two.)
A) "It starts when we put these materials into different bins at our homes or schools."
<u>B) "It also helps to save energy."</u>
<u>C) "Landfills can pollute the air and water."</u>
D) "Recycling helps fight climate change."

create inspire teach

PROMPT:	Why is recycling important?	✓ checklist
Restate the question	Recycling is important **ANSWER KEY**	✓
Answer the question	because it can help protect our environment.	✓
Cite evidence from the text	• In paragraph ___, it says… • An example from the text is… • As cited in the text,	As cited in the text, recycling can save trees, cut down on our energy use, and reduce greenhouse gas emissions.	✓
Explain how the evidence proves your answer	• Connecting this to the question, it's clear that • This part of the text reveals • This supports the idea because	This supports the idea that it is important to recycle to save our enviroment from climate change.	✓
Summarize	• The biggest idea here is • In short, • All in all,	All in all, it is crucial to our planet that we all recycle.	✓
	CAPITAL LETTER, PUNCTUATION MARKS, CORRECT SPELLING	✓

Recycling is important because it can help protect our planet. As cited in the text, recycling can save trees, cut down on our energy use, and reduce greenhouse gas emissions. This supports the idea that it is important to recycle to save our enviroment from climate change. All in all, it is crucial to our planet that we all recycle.

Name: **ANSWER KEY**

DOLPHIN TALK

Dolphins are not just playful creatures of the sea; they are also one of the smartest animals. Just like humans, dolphins use sounds and body movements to talk to one another.

The most common sounds dolphins make are called 'clicks' and 'whistles.' Dolphins use clicks to find things in the water, like fish to eat, which is known as <u>echolocation</u>. Whistles, on the other hand, are used to say hello, show excitement, or call out to other dolphins. Each dolphin has a unique whistle, which is like a name. When a dolphin hears its whistle, it responds.

Dolphins also use body movements to <u>communicate</u>. A jump out of the water can be a sign of happiness. When they slap their tails on the water, it can mean they are upset or there is danger nearby. These movements, along with sounds, make up the language that dolphins use every day.

Researchers believe that dolphins talk about more than just basic needs. They may share information, show feelings, and even make plans for the day's activities. Learning how dolphins talk to each other teaches us more about them and how they spend their days.

Dolphins communicate by using clicks, whistles, and movements, which shows how smart and social they are.

Glossary:
<u>communicate</u>- giving, receiving, and sharing information
<u>echolocation</u>- when animals use sound and echoes to find the location of objects

1. What is the main idea of the passage this passage?
A) Dolphins have a unique way of playing in the water.
<u>B) Dolphins communicate by using sounds and movements.</u>
C) Dolphins are the only creatures in the sea that can make sounds.
D) Dolphins use their tails to communicate different emotions.

2. Why might it be useful for dolphins to have a unique whistle?
A) It helps them stand out when swimming in large groups.
<u>B) It allows other dolphins to identify and respond to them.</u>
C) It scares away predators and protects younger dolphins.
D) It makes it easier for them to catch fish.

3. Part A: According to the text, how are the clicks and whistles used by dolphins different?
A) Clicks are used for playing while whistles are for echolocation.
<u>B) Clicks are for finding food and whistles are for social communication.</u>
C) Whistles are used when dolphins are alone, clicks are used in groups.
D) Clicks are made when dolphins are happy, whistles are made when they are sad.

Part B: Which sentence from the passage supports your answer to Part A? (choose 2)
<u>A) "Dolphins use clicks to find things in the water, like fish to eat."</u>
<u>B) "Each dolphin has a unique whistle, which is like a name."</u>
C) "Dolphins are not just playful creatures of the sea."
D) "A jump out of the water can be a sign of happiness."

PROMPT: How do dolphins communicate? ✓ checklist

Restate the question		Dolphins communicate **ANSWER KEY**	✓
Answer the question		by using clicks and whistles and body movements	✓
Cite evidence from the text	• The author says that… • A quote that stands out is… • As evidence, the passage says…	The author says that dolphins use clicks to find things in the water, like fish to eat, and they use whistles to say hello, show excitement, or call out to other dolphins.	✓
Explain how the evidence proves your answer	• Drawing conclusions from this, I can see that… • By stating this, the author is suggesting… • This is important because	This is important because it shows that dolphins are able to communciate with each other in different ways.	✓
Summarize	• After reading, I think… • Breaking it down, • The gist of this passage…	This gist of this passage is that dolphins are super smart animals that are able to communicate and show their emotions through sounds and body movements.	✓
	CAPITAL LETTER, PUNCTUATION MARKS, CORRECT SPELLING		✓

Dolphins communicate by using clicks, whistles and body movements. The author says that dolphins use clicks to find things in the water, like fish to eat, and they use whistles to say hello, show excitement, or call out to other dolphins. This is important because it shows that dolphins are able to communciate with each other in different ways. This gist of this passage is that dolphins are super smart animals that are able to communicate and show their emotions through sounds and body movements.

Name: _____ ANSWER KEY

THE AMAZING WORLD OF ANTS

Did you know that ants live in underground cities? These cities are super organized and busy, just like big human cities, but they're hidden beneath the ground. Let's explore this fantastic world and learn some cool facts about ant colonies!

In every ant colony, there's a special ant called the queen. She's like the mom of all the ants and lays lots and lots of eggs. There are also worker ants, who do different jobs like taking care of the queen, protecting the nest, and finding food.

Ants talk to each other by using special smells and touches. It's their way of saying, "Hey, let's work together!" Each ant has a specific role, making sure everything runs smoothly in their underground home.

What's really amazing is how ants build tunnels and rooms deep underground. They use these tunnels to keep food, stay warm or cool, and stay safe from other animals. Some ants even grow their own food by making special gardens with leaves and fungus.

Ants are like little detectives when they search for food. They follow scents and use their sharp memory to find their way back home. Teamwork is their secret superpower, making sure all the ants have enough to eat.

Ants also work together to defend their home from intruders and to build and fix their underground city. They show us how teamwork and cooperation can achieve great things!

So, next time you see ants outside, remember that they have a secret underground world full of adventure and teamwork. They might be small, but they're doing big things right beneath our f...

Ants working together to move an apple

1. What is the main idea of the passage?
A) Ants don't like living together.
B) Ants build tunnels underground.
<u>C) Ants live in organized underground colonies and work together.</u>
D) The queen is like the mom of the ants

2. What does the word "superpower" mean in the sentence "Teamwork is their secret superpower"?
<u>A) A special ability</u>
B) A building ability
C) A type of food
D) A secret code

3. What are some key characteristics of ants and their underground colonies based on the passage?
A) Ants live in underground cities.
B) The queen ant lays lots of eggs.
C) Ants communicate using special smells and touches.
<u>D) All of the above</u>

4. <u>Part A:</u> According to the passage, what is the special role of the queen ant in an ant colony?
<u>A) Laying lots of eggs</u>
B) Finding food for the colony
C) Protecting the nest from intruders
D) Building tunnels

<u>Part B:</u> What statement from the passage supports your answer from Part A?
<u>A) "The queen ant is like the mom of all the ants and lays lots and lots of eggs."</u>
B) "Ants talk to each other by using special smells and touches."
C) "Some ants even grow their own food by making special gardens with leaves and fungus."
D) "Ants follow scents and use their sharp memory to find their way back home."

create inspire teach

PROMPT:	How do ants ants help their colony?		✓ checklist
Restate the question		Ants help	✓
Answer the question		by working together to find food, build and protect their colony.	✓
Cite evidence from the text	• Highlighting this point, the text states... • From the text we can see... • Supporting this idea, the text describes...	From the text we can see each ant has a specific role, making sure everything runs smoothly in their underground home.	✓
Explain how the evidence proves your answer	• Because of this, I think • Putting this another way • This backs up my idea that	Putting this another way, ants use the tunnels that they build to keep food, stay warm or cool, and stay safe from other animals. Some ants even grow their own food by making special gardens with leaves and fungus.	✓
Summarize	• Bringing everything together, • To summarize my thoughts • After breaking it down	To summarize my thoughts, every ant has a specific job that supports helps to keep the ant colony running smoothly.	✓
	CAPITAL LETTER, PUNCTUATION MARKS, CORRECT SPELLING		✓

ANSWER KEY

Ants help by working together to find food, and to build and protect their colony. From the text we can see each ant has a specific role, making sure everything runs smoothly in their underground home. Putting this another way, ants use the tunnels that they build to keep food, stay warm or cool, and stay safe from other animals. Some ants even grow their own food by making special gardens with leaves and fungus. To summarize my thoughts, every ant has a specific job that supports helps to keep the ant colony running smoothly.

create inspire teach

Name: _____ ANSWER KEY

THE MAGIC LIBRARY ADVENTURE

Emma didn't usually like going to the library because she thought reading was really boring. But today, her mom and sister really wanted her to come with them on their weekly trip to the library. As Emma was walking between the big bookshelves, she saw a glowing book. She reached out for it, and suddenly, the shelf opened up like a door! It showed a secret room full of colorful books. Emma picked up a book called "Adventures in Storyland." When she opened the book, the room lit up with a bright light, and then, she was standing in a world just like in the storybook.

Emma was greeted by a group of talking animals - a wise owl, a jolly rabbit, and a brave cat. They told her they were characters who lived in this book, and they needed her help to solve a mystery that threatened their world. The characters explained that a fairy tale had been lost, causing chaos in Storyland. Without it, the stories were incomplete. Emma, with her love for puzzles, was excited to help.

Together with her new friends, Emma embarked on a journey. They traveled through different story worlds - from dark forests to big, sparkling castles, facing challenges and solving riddles along the way. After a journey filled with laughter and learning, Emma discovered the lost fairy tale in a forgotten corner of Storyland. The tale was about kindness and the power of words.

With the fairy tale found, Storyland was at peace again. The characters thanked Emma, and then she was transported back to the hidden room in the library. The adventure showed her that every book contains stories and lessons. Emma left the library with a new appreciation for the adventures that lay in the pages of books and that maybe reading wasn't so bad after all.

1. Part A: What did Emma do when she first arrived in the secret room in the library?
A) She read a book about castles.
<u>B) She picked up a book titled "Adventures in Storyland."</u>
C) She talked to a librarian.
D) She found a map of Storyland.

Part B: Why is Emma's action in Part A important to the story?
<u>A) It shows her curiosity and willingness to explore new things.</u>
B) It leads her to the discovery of the lost fairy tale.
C) It illustrates her initial dislike for reading.
D) It reveals her fear of magical places.

2. What was the problem in Storyland?
A) A spell was cast on the kingdom.
<u>B) A fairy tale had been lost.</u>
C) A villain was causing trouble.
D) A treasure was stolen.

3. Choose the correct event.

| Emma initially doesn't want to go to the library because she finds reading boring. | Emma opens a book called "Adventures in Storyland" and finds herself in a story world | Emma discovers the lost fairy tale in a forgotten corner of Storyland | |

A) Emma is greeted by talking animals in Storyland who need her help
B) Emma doesn't want to go to the library because she finds reading boring
<u>C) After solving the mystery, Emma returns to the library with a new appreciation for reading</u>
D) Emma, with her love for puzzles, was excited to help.

create inspire teach

			✓ checklist
PROMPT:	How has Emma's experience in the library changed her view on books and reading?		
Restate the question	Emma's experience in the library changed her view on books **ANSWER KEY**		✓
Answer the question	At first, Emma disliked reading but after her adventure in Storyland, she realized reading could be an adventure.		✓
Cite evidence from the text	• According to the text, • The text says, • It is shown in the text,	According to the text, the adventure showed her that every book contains stories and lessons. Emma left the library with a new appreciation for the adventures that lay in the pages of books and that maybe reading wasn't so bad after all.	✓
Explain how the evidence proves your answer	• When I read__, I felt… • This part seems important because, • This part shows…	This part shows that Emma's views of reading changed because of what happened at the library that day.	✓
Summarize	• Piecing everything together… • Drawing everything together… • The big lesson is…	Piecing everything together, after Emma's adventure in the library, she grew a love for reading.	✓
	CAPITAL LETTER, PUNCTUATION MARKS, CORRECT SPELLING		✓

Emma's experience in the library changed her view on books and reading. At first, Emma disliked reading but after her adventure in Storyland, she realized reading could be an adventure. According to the text, the adventure showed her that every book contains stories and lessons. Emma left the library with a new appreciation for the adventures that lay in the pages of books and that maybe reading wasn't so bad after all. This part shows that Emma's views of reading changed because of what happened at the library that day. Piecing everything together, after Emma's adventure in the library, she grew a love for reading.

create inspire teach

Name: _____ ANSWER KEY

THE LITTLE ASTRONAUT

Jamie always dreamed of exploring the stars. Every night, he gazed up at the sky, imagining what it would be like to visit other planets. One night, as he looked through his telescope, he made a wish to become an astronaut. To his surprise, a shooting star zipped across the sky, as if answering his wish. That night, Jamie had a magical dream. He found himself wearing a shiny space suit, standing in a gleaming rocket ship. "Welcome, Little Astronaut," said a friendly robot named Astro. "Ready for a space adventure?"

Their first stop was the Moon. As Jamie bounced around in the low gravity, he laughed with joy. He saw the Earth from afar, a beautiful blue marble in the vastness of space. Astro taught him about the Moon's craters and how astronauts had walked on its surface long ago.

Next, they zoomed off to Mars. The Red Planet was fascinating, with huge mountains and deep valleys. Jamie learned that Mars had the tallest volcano and the deepest canyon in the solar system. He imagined what it would be like to have a colony on Mars one day.

The rocket then took them to Saturn. Jamie was in awe of its magnificent rings. He learned that the rings were made of ice and rock. They flew close to the rings, and Jamie felt like he was in a snow globe!

As their journey ended, Jamie and Astro returned to Earth just as the sun was rising. Jamie woke up in his bed. He had traveled the solar system in his dream! From that day on, Jamie's love for space grew even more. He read books about the planets and stars, eager to learn everything he could. He knew that one day, he would become an astronaut and see the wonders of space in real life.

1. Part A: Where did Jamie first stop in his dream space adventure?
A) The Moon.
B) Mars.
C) Saturn.
D) Jupiter.

Part B: What did Jamie learn about during his stop in Part A?
A) How the Earth looked blue from the moon
B) About the Moon's craters and astronaut history.
C) Why there was no gravity on the moon
D) The temperature on the Moon.

2. What did Jamie experience and learn during his space adventure?
A) About how Saturn's rings were made of ice and rock
B) About the tallest volcano and deepest canyon on Mars.
C) About the craters on the moon
D) All of the above.

3. Choose a statement that best completes the chart.

Cause	Effect
Jamie looked through his telescope and made a wish	

A) He read a book about space
B) He gazed at the stars
C) He decided to become a scientist.
D) He had a magical dream about space.

PROMPT:	What did Jamie learn from his dream about space?	✓ checklist
Restate the question	In his dream, Jamie learned many things. **ANSWER KEY**	✓
Answer the question	One of the facts he learned was about how Saturns rings are made of ice and rock.	✓
Cite evidence from the text	• One important moment from the story… • An example from the text is… • As stated in the text,	As stated in the text, Jamie was in awe of its magnificent rings. He learned that the rings were made of ice and rock.	✓
Explain how the evidence proves your answer	• This evidence shows me, • This proves, • As you can see,	As you can see, this is an important fact about what Jamie learned in his dream. He even said when he got close to them he felt like he was in a snow globe.	✓
Summarize	• The text leaves us thinking about… • One thing is certain after reading… • Reflecting on the story…	One thing is certain after reading this, Jamie's dream taught him many things about space.	✓
	CAPITAL LETTER, PUNCTUATION MARKS, CORRECT SPELLING	✓

In his dream, Jamie learned many things. One of the facts he learned was about how Saturn's rings are made of ice and rock. As stated in the text, Jamie was in awe of its magnificent rings. He learned that the rings were made of ice and rock. As you can see, this is an important fact about what Jamie learned in his dream. He even said that when he got close to them, he felt like he was in a snow globe. One thing is certain after reading this, Jamie's dream taught him many things about space.

create inspire teach

Name: _____ **ANSWER KEY**

THE TREASURE MAP

Max was always in a hurry, never stopping to listen to anyone. One Saturday, he found an old, <u>tattered</u> map in his attic labeled "Treasure Map." Excitedly, he followed it without telling anyone, not even his best friend, Lily.

The map led Max through the town, into the forest, and finally to a big Oak tree. He started digging frantically but found nothing. Tired and disappointed, he sat down, wondering what went wrong.

Just then, Lily appeared. "I saw you rushing out with that map," she said. "I thought you might need this," handing him a magnifying glass. Looking at the map closely, Max noticed small writing he had missed before, instructing him to take ten steps left from the Oak tree.

Together, they followed the new instructions and found a small box. Inside was not gold or jewels but a note that read, "The real treasure is friendship and patience."

Max realized his haste had made him miss the true meaning of the treasure hunt. He thanked Lily for her help and promised to be more patient. From that day on, Max understood that sometimes, slowing down and having a friend by your side was more valuable than any treasure.

1. <u>Part A</u>: What mistake did Max make when he first reached the big oak tree?
A) He waited too long.
<u>B) He dug in the wrong place.</u>
C) He broke the map.
D) He called Lily for help.

<u>Part B</u>: What helped Max correct his mistake in Part A?
A) A shovel.
<u>B) Lily's magnifying glass.</u>
C) A compass.
D) A phone call.

2. In the passage, the word "tattered" is used to describe the map. Which word is a synonym for "tattered"?
A) Shiny
B) New
<u>C) Worn</u>
D) Colorful

3. Choose the correct event.

| Max finds a map and decides to follow it | → | Max digs under the big oak tree but finds nothing | → | Lily gives Max a magnifying glass and they find the note. | → | |

A) He decided not to tell Lily
B) Max followed the map into the town and the forest
<u>C) Max realizes the true meaning of the treasure hunt</u>
D) Max was disappointed when he didn't find anything

4. Which statement best represents the <u>theme</u> of the story?
A) Quick decisions lead to great discoveries.
<u>B) True friendship is more valuable than any treasure.</u>
C) Maps always lead to hidden riches.
D) Adventures are only for the brave and solitary.

create inspire teach

PROMPT: What did Max learn from his adventure with the treasure map? ✓ checklist

Restate the question		On Max's adventure with the treasure map **ANSWER KEY**	✓
Answer the question		he learned about the true meaning of friendship.	✓
Cite evidence from the text	• (The character) says… • From the dialogue, it's clear that… • A key detail from the text is…	Max says that sometimes, slowing down and having a friend by your side was more valuable than any treasure.	✓
Explain how the evidence proves your answer	• I noticed… • Because of this, I think… • An interesting part is when…	Because of this, I think that he realized his mistake in rushing to find the treasure without Lily. In the end, he wouldn't have been able to find the treasure without her.	✓
Summarize	• In the end, it's clear that… • Looking back, • It all comes down to…	In the end, it's clear that Max learned an important lesson about friendship.	✓
	CAPITAL LETTER, PUNCTUATION MARKS, CORRECT SPELLING		✓

On Max's adventure with the treasure map he learned about the true meaning of friendship. Max says that sometimes, slowing down and having a friend by your side was more valuable than any treasure. Because of this, I think that he realized his mistake in rushing to find the treasure without Lily. In the end, he wouldn't have been able to find the treasure without her. In the end, it's clear that Max learned an important lesson about friendship.

Name: _____ ANSWER KEY

THE TIME-TRAVELING HOMEWORK

Alex sat down to work on his homework where he had to write an essay about an important event in history. He chose the moon landing of 1969. As he wrote, his room began to spin, and suddenly, he found himself standing on the moon, watching Neil Armstrong take his historic first step. He was amazed by the astronauts' bravery and the silence of the lunar landscape.

In the blink of an eye, Alex's surroundings changed again. He was now in ancient Egypt, watching the workers build the Great Pyramids of Giza. He admired their methods and the massive size of the pyramids.

The next moment, Alex was taken to Italy, where he saw Leonardo da Vinci painting the Mona Lisa. He saw Leonardo's techniques and the busy streets of Florence.

Finally, Alex returned to his room, his mind buzzing with excitement. He realized that history was more than just facts; it was about the experiences of people and the impact they had on the world. With new excitement, he finished his essay, now with a different perspective on these moments in history. Alex's adventure taught him that history is a living, breathing story, filled with lessons that continue to shape our present and future.

1. Part A: What is the main idea of the passage about Alex's experience while doing his history homework?
A) Alex discovers the fun of time travel.
B) Alex learns about different historical events and figures.
C) History is more than just facts; it's about understanding people's experiences and impact.
D) Alex finishes his homework quickly.

Part B: Which detail from the passage best supports the main idea identified in Part A?
A) Alex chose to write about the moon landing of 1969.
B) Alex saw Neil Armstrong take his first step on the moon.
C) Alex admired Leonardo da Vinci's painting techniques.
D) Alex realized that history was about the experiences of people and the impact they had on the world.

2. What did Alex experience during his time-traveling adventure?
A) Witnessing the moon landing.
B) Observing the building of the Great Pyramids.
C) Seeing Leonardo da Vinci painting the Mona Lisa.
D) All of the above.

3. Choose the Cause and Effect that best supports what happened in the text.

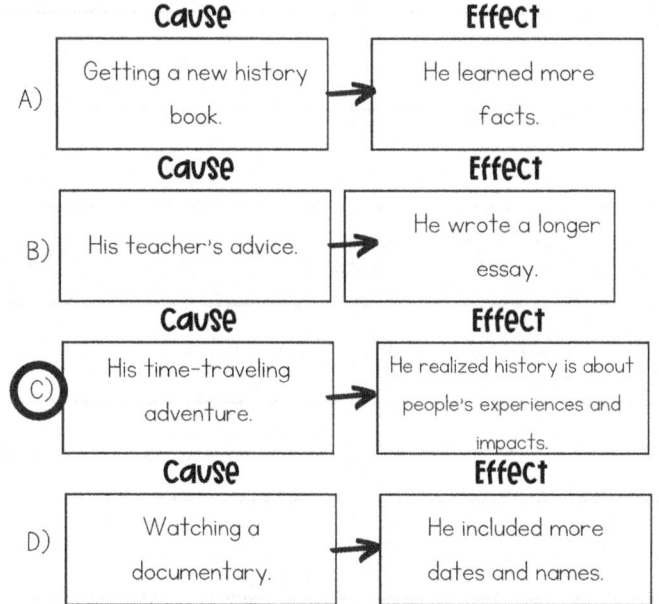

A) Cause: Getting a new history book. → Effect: He learned more facts.
B) Cause: His teacher's advice. → Effect: He wrote a longer essay.
C) Cause: His time-traveling adventure. → Effect: He realized history is about people's experiences and impacts.
D) Cause: Watching a documentary. → Effect: He included more dates and names.

create inspire teach

PROMPT: How did seeing historical events like the moon landing and the building of the Pyramids change the way Alex thinks about history?

✓ checklist

			✓
Restate the question	Seeing the historical events in person changed the way Alex thinks about history **ANSWER KEY**		✓
Answer the question	Because he knows now that history isn't just about dates and facts, it's about the people who impacted our world.		✓
Cite evidence from the text	• An instance in the story that supports this idea is... • The narrator point out... • Drawing from the text...	An instance in the story that supports this idea is when he was able to watch Neil Armstrong take his first steps on the moon.	✓
Explain how the evidence proves your answer	• This conversation shows... • What the characters did here tells us that... • From what I read, I know this is important because	From what I read, I know this is important because it taught him that history is a living, breathing story filled with lessons about bravery and never giving up.	✓
Summarize	• After reading the text, I realized... • Overall, the story teaches us... • All in all,	All in all, Alex learned an important lesson about how history is made up of amazing people and not simple dates and facts.	✓
CAPITAL LETTER, PUNCTUATION MARKS, CORRECT SPELLING			✓

Seeing the historical events in person changed the way Alex thinks about history because he now knows that history isn't just about dates and facts. It's about the people who impacted our world. An instance in the story that supports this idea is when he watched Neil Armstrong take his first steps on the moon. From what I read, I know this is important because it taught him that history is a living, breathing story filled with lessons about bravery and never giving up. All in all, Alex learned an important lesson about how history is made up of amazing people and not simple dates and facts.

create inspire teach

Name: _____ **ANSWER KEY**

JENNY'S KITE

Jenny was known in the neighborhood for having the best kite. It was a dazzling blue with a rainbow tail, and it flew higher than any other. Jenny loved showing it off at the park.

One windy day, however, disaster struck. A strong gust of wind sent her kite crashing into a tree, tearing the fabric and snapping the frame. Heartbroken, Jenny grabbed the damaged kite. She was determined to fix it, even though she had never mended one before. The repair was challenging. Jenny had to learn about different materials and techniques. She watched online videos and asked for advice at the local hobby shop. Her first few tries at fixing the kite were unsuccessful. The kite either wouldn't fly or would tumble down after a short flight.

Despite these setbacks, Jenny <u>persevered.</u> She learned to sew to repair the torn fabric and how to balance the frame properly. Each repair taught her something new about her kite and how it worked.

Other children started noticing as Jenny worked on her kite in the park. Some of them had kites with minor damages, and Jenny offered to help, sharing the skills she had learned. Together, they fixed kites of all shapes and sizes, and Jenny felt a new sense of community and friendship.

It was a triumphant moment when Jenny finally got her kite to fly again. It no longer looked perfect, with its patchwork of repairs, but it flew beautifully. Jenny realized that the true joy of kite flying wasn't in having the best kite but in the process of overcoming challenges and helping others.

1. <u>Part A:</u> What lesson does Jenny learn from her experience with the kite?
A) That only new kites can fly properly.
B) The joy of kite flying comes from owning the best kite.
<u>C) The true joy of kite flying is in overcoming challenges and helping others.</u>
D) Learning to sew is an essential skill.

<u>Part B:</u> Which detail from the passage best supports the lesson identified in Part A?
A) Jenny's kite was a dazzling blue with a rainbow tail.
B) A strong gust of wind damaged Jenny's kite.
<u>C) Jenny helped other children repair their kites.</u>
D) Jenny watched online videos to learn about kite repair.

2. In the passage, the word "persevered" describes Jenny's actions when fixing her kite. What does "persevered" mean?
A) Gave up easily.
<u>B) Worked hard even though there were challenges</u>
C) Acted quickly.
D) Asked for help.

3. Choose a statement that best completes the chart.

Cause	Effect
	The kite crashed into a tree, leading Jenny to learn new skills and help others.

A) Jenny flew the kite too high.
B) Jenny used poor-quality materials.
<u>C) A strong gust of wind came.</u>
D) Jenny had the best kite

create inspire teach

			✓ checklist
PROMPT:	What lessons did Jenny learn from the experience of fixing her kite?		
Restate the question		Jenny learned that ANSWER KEY	✓
Answer the question		persevering and helping others is very rewarding.	✓
Cite evidence from the text	• A quote that shows this... • In the beginning/middle/end of the story, it mentions... • The author mentions...	The author mentioned that Jenny realized that the true joy of kite flying wasn't in having the best kite but in the process of overcoming challenges and helping others.	✓
Explain how the evidence proves your answer	• This made me think of when... • It's interesting that the story says... • This part seems important because...	This part seems important because it shows how Jenny went from only thinking about her kite to helping others.	✓
Summarize	• To sum it all up, • In conclusion, • Without a doubt,	To sum it all up, Jenny learned about the importance of never giving up and helping other	✓
	CAPITAL LETTER, PUNCTUATION MARKS, CORRECT SPELLING		✓

Jenny learned that persevering and helping others is very rewarding. The author mentioned that Jenny realized that the true joy of kite flying wasn't in having the best kite but in the process of overcoming challenges and helping others. This part seems important because it shows how Jenny went from only thinking about her kite to helping others. To sum it all up, Jenny learned about the importance of never giving up and helping others through the experience of fixing her own kite.

create inspire teach

FALL ANSWER KEYS

Name: _____ ANSWER KEY

EMILY'S MAGICAL JOURNEY

In the town of Maplewood, where trees were bursting with shades of red, orange, and yellow during fall, Emily made an extraordinary discovery. On a chilly morning, while walking in the forest, she came across a golden leaf that shined unlike any other. As soon as she picked it up, the world changed around her.

Suddenly, Emily was in the middle of Maplewood's fall festival, but everything looked different. The people wore old-fashioned clothes, and the games they played were the ones she had only seen in history books. Emily realized the leaf had taken her back in time, so she decided to explore.

As she explored, she learned more about Maplewood's traditions. She danced to old tunes, tasted historical recipes, and listened to stories of the town's early days. The golden leaf allowed her to see how the spirit of the festival had remained, even if the celebrations had changed over the years.

As the sun set, Emily found herself back in her own time, still holding the magical leaf. She realized the true value of memories and traditions, and how they connect generations of people in Maplewood.

1. Why did Emily decide to explore the old version of Maplewood's fall festival?
a) She was curious about the historical recipes.
b) <u>The golden leaf had taken her back in time.</u>
c) She wanted to play the old games.
d) The people in old-fashioned clothes invited her.

2. What is the main lesson or moral of the story?
a) Magic can be found in forests.
b) <u>Memories and traditions connect generations of people.</u>
c) Old games are better than new ones.
d) Golden leaves are rare.

3. In the story, the word <u>"extraordinary"</u> is used to describe Emily's discovery. What does "extraordinary" mean in this context?
a) Ordinary
b) Usual
c) <u>Very special or unusual</u>
d) Common

4. From whose point of view is the story told?
a) Emily's
b) The golden leaf's
c) The people of Maplewood
d) <u>A third-person narrator</u>

5. How has the celebration of Maplewood's fall festival changed over the years based on Emily's journey?
a) The festival has completely stopped.
b) The spirit of the festival has not remained the same, but the celebrations have changed.
c) The games played are exactly the same.
d) <u>People no longer wear old-fashioned clothes.</u>

create inspire teach

PROMPT:	How did Emily's experience at the old Maplewood festival help her understand the town's traditions and the importance of memories?		✓ checklist
Restate the question	Emily was able to understand the town's traditions and important memories	**ANSWER KEY**	✓
Answer the question	when she went back in time.		✓
Cite evidence from the text	• According to the text, • The text says, • It is shown in the text,	According to the text, she danced to old tunes, tasted historical recipes, and listened to stories of the town's early days.	✓
Explain how the evidence proves your answer	• When I read___, I felt… • This part seems important because, • This part shows…	This part seems important because she was see how the spirit of the festival had remained, even if the celebrations had changed over the years.	✓
Summarize	• Piecing everything together… • Drawing everything together… • The big lesson is…	Piecing everything together, Emily was able to understand the true value of memories and traditions and how they connect generations of people in Maplewood.	✓
	CAPITAL LETTER, PUNCTUATION MARKS, CORRECT SPELLING		✓

Emily was able to understand the town's traditions and important memories when she went back in time. According to the text, when she went to the old festival, she danced to old tunes, tasted historical recipes, and listened to stories of the town's early days. This part seems important because it shows how the spirit of the festival had remained, even if the celebrations had changed over the years. Piecing everything together, Emily was able to understand the true value of memories and traditions and how they connect generations of people in Maplewood.

create inspire teach

Name: _____ ANSWER KEY

THE ENCHANTED PUMPKIN PATCH

In the small town of Everglen, children talked about a hidden, magical pumpkin patch. Tucked behind the tall oak trees was a pumpkin patch with a pumpkin that shimmered in the moonlight. The children said that this magical pumpkin granted wishes, but only to the children who believed in its magic.

One crisp afternoon, Mia and Jake were walking in the woods and found the hidden patch with the shimmering pumpkin. Amazed, Mia touched the pumpkin, and it began to glow even brighter. Remembering the stories, Mia and Jake made a wish. Instead of wishing for toys or treats, they wished to help others in their town.

To their astonishment, the pumpkin gave them a bag of golden seeds. Each seed, when planted, would instantly grow and produce fruits or vegetables. With joy and determination, Jake and Mia went around Everglen, planting the magical seeds and turning empty land into huge gardens.

As winter approached, thanks to Mia and Jake's selfless acts, no one in Everglen went hungry. The town was filled with gratitude and warmth. While the enchanted pumpkin remained a secret, its spirit of giving lived on in the hearts of the townspeople, especially Mia and Jake.

1. <u>Part A</u>: What was special about the shimmering pumpkin in the hidden patch?
a) It could dance and sing.
<u>b) It granted wishes to children who believed in its magic.</u>
c) It glowed only during the day.
d) It was the smallest pumpkin in Everglen.

<u>Part B</u>: Which sentence from the passage best supports your answer to Part A?
<u>a) "In the small town of Everglen, children talked about a hidden, magical pumpkin patch."</u>
b) "On a chilly afternoon, Mia and Jake were walking in the woods..."
c) "Amazed, Mia touched the shimmering pumpkin, and it began to glow even brighter."
d) "Tucked behind the tall oak trees was a pumpkin patch with a pumpkin that shimmered in the moonlight."

2. In the passage, the word "astonishment" most likely means:
a) Sadness
b) Anger
<u>c) Surprise or amazement</u>
d) Boredom

3. Whose point of view is the story told from?
a) Mia's.
b) Jake's.
c) The pumpkin's.
<u>d) A third-person narrator.</u>

4. Which of the following is a theme present in the story?
a) The magic of nature.
b) The value of selflessness and community.
c) The importance of belief.
<u>d) All of the above.</u>

create inspire teach

PROMPT:	How did Mia and Jake's discovery of the enchanted pumpkin change the lives of the people in Everglen?	✓ checklist
Restate the question	Mia and Jake's discovery of the enchanted pumpkin changed the lives of the people in Everglen **ANSWER KEY**	✓
Answer the question	because they were plant seeds which were used to feed people in the community throughout winter.	✓
Cite evidence from the text	• One important moment from the story... • An example from the text is... • As stated in the text,	As stated in the text, each seed, when planted, would instantly grow and produce fruits or vegetables.	✓
Explain how the evidence proves your answer	• This evidence shows me, • This proves, • As you can see,	As you can see, thanks to Mia and Jake's selfless acts, no one in Everglen went hungry.	✓
Summarize	• The text leaves us thinking about... • One thing is certain after reading... • Reflecting on the story...	One thing is certain after reading, because of Jake, Mia, and the magic pumpkin, many people were able to enjoy winter.	✓
CAPITAL LETTER, PUNCTUATION MARKS, CORRECT SPELLING		✓

Mia and Jake's discovery of the enchanted pumpkin changed the lives of the people in Everglen because they were plant seeds which were used to feed people in the community throughout winter. As stated in the text, each seed, when planted, would instantly grow and produce fruits or vegetables. As you can see, thanks to Mia and Jake's selfless acts, no one in Everglen went hungry. One thing is certain after reading, because of Jake, Mia, and the magic pumpkin, many people were able to enjoy winter.

create inspire teach

Name: _____ **ANSWER KEY**

A SWEET ADVENTURE

In the heart of the busy town of Harvestville, Mrs. Maple's bakery was known for its delicious pies. One day, two of her most famous pies – Apple Andy and Pumpkin Patty – found themselves side by side on the window sill, basking in the afternoon sun.

"You know, Patty," began Andy, with a mischievous glint in his baked crusty eyes, "I've always wondered what lies beyond this bakery." Patty giggled, "Oh, Andy! Always daydreaming! But I have also wondered about the world outside." As the two pies chatted, a gust of wind blew through the open window, lifting the checkered cloth that covered them. Seeing the opportunity, Andy and Patty hopped off the sill and began their adventure.

The two pies rolled down the streets of Harvestville, experiencing the world in a way they never imagined. They rolled past children playing in parks, over bridges with streams flowing underneath, and through fields filled with the aroma of fall. But it wasn't all fun and games. At one point, a hungry squirrel tried to get a nibble of Andy, and later, a crow tried to get Patty. Each time, they managed to escape, thanks to their quick thinking and teamwork. After hours of exploration, the pies found themselves on a hill overlooking Harvestville. The town lights twinkled, and from the distance, they could hear the familiar jingle of Mrs. Maple's bakery.

Patty sighed, "It's been an amazing journey, Andy. But I think it's time we head back home. I miss Mrs. Maple." Andy nodded, "You're right, Patty. There's no place like Mrs. Maple's bakery. Let's roll back before she misses us too!" Using the slope of the hill to their advantage, they rolled back into town and jumped onto their familiar spot at the window sill just as Mrs. Maple was closing her shop.

The next morning, a little boy exclaimed, "Look, Mom! It seems like the apple and pumpkin pies have been on some adventure. They're all covered in leaves and twigs!" Mrs. Maple laughed, "Oh, the tales our pies could tell if they could speak!"

As the sun shone on another beautiful day in Harvestville, Apple Andy and Pumpkin Patty shared a secret smile, thinking about their fun adventure but also being happy that they are home.

1. <u>Part A</u>: Why did Apple Andy and Pumpkin Patty decide to leave the bakery?
a) They were not tasty.
<u>b) They wanted to see the world outside.</u>
c) Mrs. Maple asked them to leave.
d) They were sold to a customer.

<u>Part B</u>: Which sentence from the passage best supports your answer to Part A?
a) "Mrs. Maple's bakery was renowned for its delectable pies."
<u>b) "I've always wondered what lies beyond this bakery."</u>
c) "Mrs. Maple laughed, 'Oh, the tales our pies could tell if they could speak!'"
d) "The next morning, a little boy exclaimed, 'Look, Mom!'"

2. The phrase "basking in the afternoon sun" most likely means:
a) Getting baked again.
b) Feeling very hot.
<u>c) Enjoying the warmth and light of the sun.</u>
d) Talking under the sun.

3. Which part of the story signifies the climax of the pies' adventure?
a) When they are sitting on the window sill.
b) When they roll down the streets of Harvestville.
c) When they escape from the squirrel and the crow.
<u>d) When they reach the hill overlooking Harvestville</u>

create inspire teach
159

PROMPT:	How did the Patty and Andy's beliefs change throughout the text?	✓ checklist
Restate the question	Patty and Andy's beliefs changed throughout the story **ANSWER KEY**	✓
Answer the question	because at first, they wanted to explore the world outside but then they missed the bakery.	✓
Cite evidence from the text	• (The character) says... • From the dialogue, it's clear that... • A key detail from the text is...	Pumpkin Patty said, "It's been an amazing journey, Andy. But I think it's time we head back home. I miss Mrs. Maple."	✓
Explain how the evidence proves your answer	• I noticed... • Because of this, I think... • An interesting part is when...	An interesting part is when they shared a secret smile as they thought about their fun adventure but also being happy that they are home.	✓
Summarize	• In the end, it's clear that... • Looking back, • It all comes down to...	In the end, it's clear they had fun on their adventure but also realized that the bakery is where they belonged.	✓
	CAPITAL LETTER, PUNCTUATION MARKS, CORRECT SPELLING	✓

Patty and Andy's beliefs changed throughout the story because at first, they wanted to explore the world outside but then they missed the bakery. Pumpkin Patty said, "It's been an amazing journey, Andy. But I think it's time we head back home. I miss Mrs. Maple." An interesting part is when they shared a secret smile at the end as they thought about their fun adventure but also being happy that they were home. In the end, it's clear they had fun on their adventure but also realized that the bakery is where they belonged.

create inspire teach

Name: _____ ANSWER KEY

THE PINECONE'S PURPOSE: A FALL ADVENTURE

In the heart of Whispering Woods, fall was everyone's favorite season. The leaves turned golden, and the air was crisp. Among the forest's inhabitants was Peter the Pinecone, who lived high up in the oldest pine tree. Unlike other pinecones, Peter often felt out of place and wondered about his purpose.

One brisk morning, a gust of wind carried him away, and he landed in a clearing surrounded by different creatures. Curious eyes stared at him: from a curious rabbit to a clever crow named Clara.

Seeing Peter's confusion, Clara fluttered down and said, "Ah, young Pinecone, everyone in this forest has a purpose. Do you know yours?"

Peter shook his head. "I've always wondered why I exist. I'm not as shiny as dew or as lively as leaves."

An elderly mushroom named Mortimer overheard and chuckled, "Oh, dear Peter! Pinecones, like you, have a grand purpose! You protect and house the seeds of the pine tree. You make sure the forest grows and thrives. When the time is right, you release the seeds, giving birth to new trees."

Peter blinked in surprise. "I do that?"

Clara nodded, "Indeed! And in fall, many pinecones begin their journey, making space for new pinecones to take your place when spring comes."

Peter's heart swelled with pride. With the help of his new friends, he embarked on an adventure to find the perfect spot to release his seeds, ensuring the legacy of the Whispering Woods continued.

The tale of Peter's journey spread throughout the forest, reminding every creature of the beauty of fall and the importance of understanding one's purpose.

1. Part A: What is the main role of a pinecone in the forest, according to the passage?
a) To be a plaything for forest creatures.
b) To fall during autumn.
c) To protect and carry the seeds of the pine tree.
d) To give shade to small animals.

Part B: Which statement from the passage best supports your answer to Part A?
a) "In the heart of Whispering Woods, fall was everyone's favorite season."
b) "Peter often felt out of place and wondered about his purpose."
c) "Pinecones, like you, have a grand purpose! You protect and house the seeds of the pine tree, ensuring the forest grows and thrives."
d) "The tale of Peter's journey spread throughout the forest..."

2. What are the themes or messages of the story?
a) Every being in nature has its unique role.
b) Recognizing your importance can bring joy.
c) Being part of a community helps us learn more about ourselves.
d) All of the above.

3. In the passage, the term "legacy" most likely refers to:
a) A long-standing tradition.
b) An old tale of the forest.
c) Something that is passed down through generations.
d) A path in the Whispering Woods.

4. How did Peter's feelings change throughout the story?
a) He was always confident and never questioned his purpose.
b) He started off curious and ended up proud of his role.
c) He felt the same about his purpose from the beginning to the end.
d) He was sad throughout the entire story.

create inspire teach

PROMPT: How did the Whispering Woods community help Peter the Pinecone understand his importance and role in the forest?

✓ checklist

Restate the question	The Whispering Woods community help Peter the Pinecone understand his importance and role in the forest	**ANSWER KEY**	✓
Answer the question		by explaining what how a pinecone helps the forest.	✓
Cite evidence from the text	• An instance in the story that supports this idea is... • The narrator point out... • Drawing from the text...	An instance in the story that supports this idea is when Martimer the mushroom said "You protect and house the seeds of the pine tree. You make sure the forest grows and thrives."	✓
Explain how the evidence proves your answer	• This conversation shows... • What the characters did here tells us that... • From what I read, I know this is important because	What this characters did here tells us that he wanted to help the pinecone find his purpose.	✓
Summarize	• After reading the text, I realized... • Overall, the story teaches us... • All in all,	All in all, the story teaches us that our community can help us figure out who we are.	✓
	CAPITAL LETTER, PUNCTUATION MARKS, CORRECT SPELLING		✓

The Whispering Woods community help Peter the Pinecone understand his importance and role in the forest by explaining what how a pinecone helps the forest. An instance in the story that supports this idea is when Martimer the mushroom said "You protect and house the seeds of the pine tree. You make sure the forest grows and thrives." What this character did here tells us that he wanted to help the pinecone find his purpose. All in all, the story teaches us that our community can help us figure out who we are.

create inspire teach

Name: _____ **ANSWER KEY**

GRANDMA'S APPLE PIE

As the leaves began to cover the yard, I knew it was time for our annual pie-making tradition. Every fall, my Grandma Ella and I would spend a day making her famous apple pie.

One sunny afternoon, I went to her cottage and was greeted by the delightful aroma of spices. "Ready for our pie day?" Grandma Ella asked, her eyes sparkling with excitement. "Always!" I replied.

We started by picking apples from the old tree in her garden. Each apple was a memory, a story of past seasons. As we chose the juiciest ones, Grandma shared tales of her childhood when she and her sisters would climb the tree, competing to pick the highest apple.

Back in the kitchen, I watched as Grandma skillfully peeled and sliced the apples. She then handed me her special spice mix, a secret recipe passed down through generations. "Remember, a pinch of this and a handful of love," she would always say.

As the pie baked, the house filled with an irresistible aroma. I cherished these moments – the warmth, the stories, and the bond that only strengthened over time.

Finally, with the pie cooling on the windowsill, we sat on the porch, sipping hot cider. As the sun set, painting the sky with hues of orange and pink, I realized that it wasn't just about baking a pie. It was about the stories, the memories, and the love that went into it. Grandma Ella's apple pie was a slice of our shared history, and I hoped to continue the tradition for years to come.

1. Why did the narrator look forward to fall every year?
a) Because she loved watching the leaves change colors.
b) To participate in the annual pie-making tradition with Grandma Ella.
c) Because fall was the only time she visited her grandma.
d) Because she loved apple picking.

2. What did Grandma Ella's special spice mix represent?
a) Just another ingredient for the pie.
b) A secret that the narrator wasn't allowed to share.
c) A family recipe passed down through generations.
d) Something she bought from a special store.

3. From whose point of view is the story told?
a) Grandma Ella's
b) The apple tree's
c) A third-person observer
d) The granddaughter's

4. In the passage, the phrase "a slice of our shared history" most likely means:
a) The pie was very old.
b) The pie-making process was a reflection of their family traditions and memories.
c) They always shared a single slice of pie.
d) The pie reminded them of a history lesson.

5. If there was an illustration showing the pie-making process in the kitchen, what might you expect to see based on details from the text?
a) Grandma Ella reading a book.
b) The narrator peeling and slicing apples alone.
c) A messy kitchen with flour everywhere.
d) Grandma Ella skillfully handling apples and the narrator with a spice mix.

create inspire teach

			✓ checklist
PROMPT:	What lessons did the narrator learn from making pie with grandma every fall?		
Restate the question	The narrator learned that	**ANSWER KEY**	✓
Answer the question	the day wasn't only about pie making, it was also about the stories, the memories, and the love that went into it.		✓
Cite evidence from the text	• A quote that shows this. • In the beginning/middle/end of the story, it mentions… • The author mentions…	A quote that shows this is "I cherished these moments – the warmth, the stories, and the bond that only strengthened over time.	✓
Explain how the evidence proves your answer	• This made me think of when… • It's interesting that the story says… • This part seems important because…	This part seems important because it shows that even though they are making pies, she is learning so much more than that.	✓
Summarize	• To sum it all up, • In conclusion, • Without a doubt,	Without a doubt, the narrator learned about the traditions that went into creating Grandma's apple pie.	✓
	CAPITAL LETTER, PUNCTUATION MARKS, CORRECT SPELLING		✓

The narrator learned that the day wasn't only about pie making, it was also about the stories, the memories, and the love that went into it. A quote that shows this is "I cherished these moments – the warmth, the stories, and the bond that only strengthened over time." This part seems important because it shows that even though they are making pies, she is learning so much more than that. Without a doubt, the narrator learned about the traditions that went into creating Grandma's apple pie.

create inspire teach

Name: _____ ANSWER KEY

FALL LEAVES AND THEIR NEW COLORS

    Every year, trees start putting on a beautiful show of colors. Have you ever wondered why leaves change their colors during the fall? It's all thanks to a little science and nature's way of getting ready for the winter.

    Inside every leaf is a special substance called chlorophyll (klor-o-fill). Chlorophyll is what gives leaves their green color during spring and summer. But here's the fascinating part: as trees sense less sunlight and feel the cooler temperatures of the fall, they start conserving their energy for the upcoming winter. This means they produce less chlorophyll. As the days get shorter and cooler, trees get a signal that it's time to get ready for winter, and the chlorophyll starts to break down and fade away. When this happens, other hidden colors in the leaves, which were always there but overshadowed by the green, begin to shine through!

    Some trees, like oak trees, have leaves that turn deep red or brown. Maple trees show off bright reds, sunny oranges, or golden yellows. And aspen trees? Their leaves become a shimmering gold!

    So, the next time you see the beautiful fall colors, you'll know it's the trees saying, "Winter is coming, but first, here's a colorful show!"

1. <u>Part A:</u> What is the main idea of this passage?
a. Trees have a special substance called chlorophyll in their leaves.
b. The days become shorter and cooler in the winter.
<u>c. Trees show off different colors to signal the approach of winter.</u>
d. Maple and oak trees are the most common types of trees.

<u>Part B:</u> Which sentence from the passage best supports your answer from Part A?
a. "Inside every leaf is a special substance called chlorophyll (klor-o-fill)."
b. "As the days get shorter and cooler in the fall, trees get a signal that it's time to get ready for winter."
c. "Maple trees show off bright reds, sunny oranges, or golden yellows."
<u>d. "So, the next time you see the beautiful fall colors, you'll know it's the trees saying, 'Winter is coming, but first, here's a colorful show!'"</u>

2. Choose the word that best supports the meaning of the underlined word.

"But here's the fascinating part: as trees sense less sunlight and feel the cooler temperatures of the fall, they start <u>conserving</u> their energy for the upcoming winter."

a. wasting
b. ignoring
<u>c. saving</u>
d. using

3. According to the passage, what happens to chlorophyll when the days get shorter in the fall?
a. It makes the leaves turn green.
<u>b. It starts to break down and fade away.</u>
c. It creates new colors in the leaves.
d. It makes the leaves fall off the trees.

4. Why do you think it's important for trees to prepare for winter?
a. So they can grow fruits.
<u>b. To protect themselves from cold and harsh conditions.</u>
c. To show off their beautiful colors.
d. To ensure they get enough sunlight.

create inspire teach   165

PROMPT:	Why do leaves change colors in the fall?	✓ checklist
Restate the question	Leaves change colors in the fall **ANSWER KEY**	✓
Answer the question	because trees start to save energy as they sense less sunlight and cooler temperatures.	✓
Cite evidence from the text	• According to the text, • The text says, • It is shown in the text,	According to the texts, when trees save their energy, the make less chlorophyll; the substance that turns leaves green.	✓
Explain how the evidence proves your answer	• This evidence shows me, • This proves, • As you can see,	This evidence shows me that the leaves change colors in the fall as a result of less chlorophyll in the leaves.	✓
Summarize	• To sum it all up, • In conclusion, • Without a doubt,	Without a doubt, we all know the the changing leaves are beautiful but now we know how it happens!	✓
	CAPITAL LETTER, PUNCTUATION MARKS, CORRECT SPELLING	✓

Leaves change colors in the fall because trees start to save energy as the sunlight gets shorter and the temperatures get cooler. According to the texts, when trees save their energy, the make less chlorophyll; the substance that turns leaves green. This evidence shows me that the leaves change colors in the fall as a result of less chlorophyll in the leaves. Without a doubt, we all know the the changing leaves are beautiful but now we know how it happens!

create inspire teach

Name: __ANSWER KEY__

HARVEST PARTIES FROM AROUND THE GLOBE

All around the world, people love to celebrate the foods they've grown. These celebrations, called harvest festivals, happen when crops are ready to be picked and eaten. Let's take a look at a few!

In America, people celebrate <u>Thanksgiving</u>. Families gather around big tables filled with turkey, corn, and pumpkin pies. They give thanks for the good things that have happened throughout the year.

Over in China, there's the <u>Mid-Autumn Festival</u>. People admire the full moon and share round mooncakes with their loved ones. These sweet cakes symbolize togetherness and harmony.

Germany has a lively celebration named <u>Oktoberfest</u>. Although it starts in September, it's all about October! People come together to dance, sing, and enjoy large mugs of apple cider and other drinks. Delicious sausages and pretzels are often on the menu too!

Let's not forget India and its vibrant <u>Diwali</u> festival. Known as the Festival of Lights, it's a time when homes are decorated with oil lamps and candles. Families come together to feast on sweets, exchange gifts, and thank the goddess Lakshmi for a successful harvest.

Different places, different parties, but one common reason: to celebrate the food that the Earth has given!

1. Part A: What is the main purpose of this passage?
a. To describe different dances from around the world.
<u>b. To explain how different cultures celebrate harvest season.</u>
c. To share recipes from different harvest festivals.
d. To discuss the history of harvest celebrations.

Part B: Which sentence from the passage best supports your answer from Part A?
<u>a. "All around the world, people love to celebrate the foods they've grown."</u>
b. "In America, people celebrate Thanksgiving."
c. "These sweet cakes symbolize togetherness and harmony."

2. Why do different cultures have harvest festivals?
a. To show off their dance moves.
b. To enjoy the cold winter weather.
<u>c. To celebrate the food the Earth has provided.</u>
d. To exchange gifts with neighbors.

3. How do the photos help you understand more about each harvest party?
a. They show what the author looks like
b. They show where each harvest party takes place
c. They show why people celebrate the harvest
<u>d. They show the food each culture enjoys</u>

create inspire teach

PROMPT: How do different cultures celebrate the harvest season?			✓ checklist
Restate the question	Different cultures celebrate the harvest season	**ANSWER KEY**	✓
Answer the question		in many different ways.	✓
Cite evidence from the text	• The author states.. • In the passage, it mentioned that... • From the reading, I learned...	The author states that in the America, people celebrate Thanksgiving where Turkey is the main dish and in Germany they celebrate Octoberfest where sausages and pretzels are on the menu.	✓
Explain how the evidence proves your answer	• This demonstrates that • From this, we can understand that • This detail shed light on	This detail sheds light on the different way people celebrate the harvest season around the world.	✓
Summarize	• In a nutshell, • After reading, I know... • The main thing to remember	The main thing to remember is that each culture has their own way of celebrating the food the Earth has given us!	✓
CAPITAL LETTER, PUNCTUATION MARKS, CORRECT SPELLING			✓

Different cultures celebrate the harvest season in many different ways. The author states that in the America, people celebrate Thanksgiving where Turkey is the main dish and in Germany they celebrate Octoberfest where sausages and pretzels are on the menu. This detail sheds light on the different way people celebrate the harvest season around the world. The main thing to remember is that each culture has their own way of celebrating the food the Earth has given us!

Name: _____ ANSWER KEY

JOURNEYS OF FALL: THE MIGRATIONS OF THE ANIMAL WORLD

Every fall, while humans are sipping hot cocoa and watching leaves fall, a different kind of magic happens in the animal world. Thousands of creatures, from the tiniest insects to the largest mammals, embark on epic journeys. This incredible movement from one place to another is called <u>migration.</u>

Many birds, like the Arctic tern and the red knot, fly thousands of miles to escape the cold and find food. They travel from the icy northern regions to the warmer southern lands, using the stars, the Earth's magnetic field, and even landmarks to guide their way. These trips aren't just for a holiday; they're crucial for their survival. But it's not an easy flight; they face challenges like bad weather, hunters, and even getting lost!

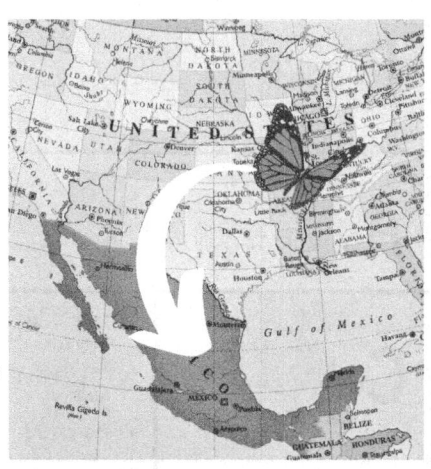

The monarch butterfly travels up to 3,000 miles as they travel from North America to Central Mexico during the fall.

While many birds take to the skies, some animals and insects travel by land or sea. One of the most amazing insects is the Monarch butterfly. These insects fly up to 3,000 miles from North America to Central Mexico to avoid the cold winter. Imagine something so tiny going such a long distance! Their journey is made even more magical as they travel in groups, filling the sky with their orange and black wings.

Why do these animals go through such great lengths and face so many dangers? For many, it's about survival. They migrate to find food and to find suitable homes where they can grow.

So, as you cozy up this fall, think about the animals who will travel far and face tough journeys.

1. According to the passage, why do animals migrate?
a. To enjoy the scenery.
b. To escape hunters.
c. To meet other species.
<u>d. To find food and homes.</u>

2. What methods do birds use to guide their migration path?
a. Using the stars.
b. Following the Earth's magnetic field.
c. Recognizing landmarks.
<u>d. All of the above.</u>

3. What does the caption tell us about the Monarch Butterfly?
a. What they look like
b. What they eat
<u>c. About their migration</u>

4. <u>Part A</u>: What is the main idea of the passage?
a. The Monarch butterfly has a unique color pattern.
<u>b. Many animals move from one place to another during fall.</u>
c. Birds use various methods to guide their migration path.
d. Migration is an easy journey for animals.

<u>Part B</u>: Which sentence from the passage best supports your answer from Part A?
<u>a. "Every fall, while humans are sipping hot cocoa and watching leaves fall, a different kind of magic happens in the animal world."</u>
b. "Many birds, like the Arctic tern and the red knot, fly thousands of miles to escape the cold and find food."
c. "One of the most amazing insects is the Monarch butterfly."
d. "They migrate to find food and to find suitable homes where they can thrive."

create inspire teach

PROMPT:	Why is it important for animals and insects to migrate during the fall?	✓ checklist
Restate the question	It is important for animals and insects to migrate during the fall **ANSWER KEY**	✓
Answer the question	to find food and homes during the winter.	✓
Cite evidence from the text	• In paragraph ___, it says... • An example from the text is... • As cited in the text,	In paragraph 2, it says many birds, like the Arctic tern and the red knot, fly thousands of miles to escape the cold and find food.	✓
Explain how the evidence proves your answer	• Connecting this to the question, it's clear that • This part of the text reveals • This supports the idea because	This supports the idea that animals need to migrate many miles to be able ti survive the cold winter months.	✓
Summarize	• The biggest idea here is • In short, • All in all,	All in all, animals and insects take long and hard journeys to be able to survive.	✓
	CAPITAL LETTER, PUNCTUATION MARKS, CORRECT SPELLING	✓

It is important for animals and insects to migrate during the fall to find food and homes during the winter. In paragraph 2, it says many birds, like the Arctic tern and the red knot, fly thousands of miles to escape the cold and find food. This supports the idea that animals need to migrate many miles to be able to survive the cold winter months. All in all, animals and insects take long and hard journeys to be able to survive.

Name: _____ ANSWER KEY

CORN MAZES: A FALL ADVENTURE!

Imagine walking through tall paths of corn, turning left and right, trying to find your way out. That's the fun of a corn maze! But how did this cool fall activity begin?

In the 1990's, people noticed that big fields of corn could be more than just food. They thought, "Why not turn them into giant puzzles for everyone to enjoy?" And just like that, the first corn mazes were born! These mazes quickly became a fun way to enjoy the crisp fall air.

Creating a corn maze is like drawing a big picture, but on a field! Farmers first decide on a design. It could be anything - a giant pumpkin, a spooky ghost, or even a castle! Once they have an idea, they wait for the corn to grow a little. When it's just the right height, they begin to cut out paths. Some farmers even use drones to help them!

Did you know that there are some super-sized corn mazes out there? One of the biggest corn mazes in the world is as big as 40 football fields! And some mazes are so tricky that they even give you a map at the start.

So, the next time you put on your boots and run into a corn maze, think of all the fun and history behind it. It's not just a game; it's a tradition that has been around for many years!

The first corn maze was created in Pennsylvania in the 1993. Now some mazes are created using GPS and drones!

1. Which sentence from the passage best supports that this passage is about the fun facts and history of corn mazes.?
a. "A long time ago, people noticed that big fields of corn could be more than just food."
b. "Creating a corn maze is like drawing a big picture, but on a field!"
c. "One of the biggest corn mazes in the world covered a space as big as 40 football fields!"
d. "It's not just a game; it's a tradition that has been around for many, many years!"

2. Which statement is true according to the passage?
a. Corn mazes are only made in fall.
b. The first corn mazes were made hundreds of years ago.
c. Some corn mazes are as big as 40 football fields.
d. All of the above.

3. Part A: Why were corn mazes originally created?
a. For farmers to earn money.
b. To feed the local animals.
c. For everyone to enjoy as a fun activity.
d. To store food for winter.

Part B: Which sentence from the passage best supports your answer from Part A?
a. "Imagine walking through tall paths of corn, turning left and right, trying to find your way out."
b. "They thought, 'Why not turn them into giant puzzles for everyone to enjoy?'"
c. "Creating a corn maze is like drawing a big picture, but on a field!"
d. "Some farmers even use drones to help them!"

create inspire teach

PROMPT:	How do farmers design corn mazes?		✓ checklist
Restate the question		Farmers design corn mazes **ANSWER KEY**	✓
Answer the question		by creating the design, letting the corn grow, and then cutting out the paths.	✓
Cite evidence from the text	• The author shows that.. • A quote that stands out is… • As evidence, the passage says…	As evidence, the passage says now some corn mazes are created using GPS and drones.	✓
Explain how the evidence proves your answer	• Drawing conclusions from this, I can see that… • By stating this, the author is suggesting… • This is important because	This is important because it shows how technology has changed how farmers are creating corn mazes.	✓
Summarize	• After reading, I think… • Breaking it down, • The gist of this passage…	The gist of this passage is that farmers take time to create corn mazes.	✓
	CAPITAL LETTER, PUNCTUATION MARKS, CORRECT SPELLING		✓

Farmers design corn mazes by creating the design, letting the corn grow, and then cutting out the paths. As evidence, the passage says now some corn mazes are created using GPS and drones. This is important because it shows how technology has changed how farmers are creating corn mazes. The gist of this passage is that there is a lot of fun and history behind the creation of corn mazes.

create inspire teach

Name: __ANSWER KEY__

SCARECROWS: THE WATCHFUL PROTECTORS OF FALL

Long before there were big machines and advanced technology to help farmers, there were scarecrows. Standing tall in fields, with clothes flapping in the wind, these straw-filled figures have a job: to scare away birds and protect the crops.

The idea of the scarecrow has been around for a very long time. Different countries had their own versions. In ancient Egypt, farmers made wooden scarecrows to protect wheat fields from quail. In Japan, they used bamboo frames and old rags.

But why are scarecrows linked with fall? Fall is harvest time. It's when fruits, vegetables, and grains are ready to be picked. And it's also when birds are looking for food. So, farmers put scarecrows in fields to keep the hungry birds away.

Over time, scarecrows became more than just farm helpers. People began making them for fun, using colorful clothes and creative designs. Today, during fall, many towns have scarecrow festivals. Families come together to create the most unique and funniest scarecrows. They have truly become a symbol of the season!

Scarecrows have been used for over 3,000 years. The first scarecrows were in ancient Egypt, and used to protect wheat fields along the Nile River from flocks of quail.

1. Part A: What is the main purpose of scarecrows?
a. To look funny and entertain people.
b. To be used in festivals.
c. To scare away birds and protect crops.
d. To be a symbol of ancient Egypt.

Part B: Which sentence from the passage best supports your answer from Part A?
a. "Standing tall in fields, with clothes flapping in the wind, these straw-filled figures have a job: to scare away birds and protect the crops."
b. "Over time, scarecrows became more than just farm helpers."
c. "Today, during fall, many towns have scarecrow festivals."
d. "In Japan, they used bamboo frames and old rags."

2. Part A: Over time, how has the use of scarecrows changed?
a. They became symbols of ancient cultures.
b. They are now only used to scare birds.
c. They became part of fall celebrations and festivals.
d. They are considered bad luck.

Part B: Which sentence from the passage supports your answer from Part A?
a. "In ancient Egypt, farmers made wooden scarecrows to protect wheat fields from quail."
b. "But why are scarecrows linked with fall? Fall is harvest time."
c. "Today, during fall, many towns have scarecrow festivals."
d. "Standing tall in fields, with clothes flapping in the wind, these straw-filled figures have a job."

3. Which statement is TRUE based on the passage?
a. Scarecrows were first made in Japan.
b. Only birds are scared of scarecrows.
c. Scarecrows are mainly made from straw.
d. All of the above.

create inspire teach

			✓ checklist
PROMPT:	Why are scarecrows important for farming?		
Restate the question		Scarecrows are important for farming **ANSWER KEY**	✓
Answer the question		because the scare away birds and protect the crops.	✓
Cite evidence from the text	• Highlighting this point, the text states… • From the text we can see… • Supporting this idea, the text describes…	From the text we can see that farmers put scarecrows in fields to keep the hungry birds away.	✓
Explain how the evidence proves your answer	• Because of this, I think • Putting this another way • This backs up my idea that	Putting this another way, scarecrows standing tall in fields with clothes flapping in the wind helps to protect the crop from animals.	✓
Summarize	• Bringing everything together, • To summarize my thoughts • After breaking it down	After breaking it down, scarecrows help to protect crops from birds that want to eat them.	✓
	CAPITAL LETTER, PUNCTUATION MARKS, CORRECT SPELLING		✓

Scarecrows are important for farming because the scare away birds and protect the crops. From the text we can see that farmers put scarecrows in fields to keep the hungry birds away. Putting this another way, scarecrows standing tall in fields with clothes flapping in the wind helps to protect the crop from animals. After breaking it down, scarecrows help to protect crops from birds that want to eat them.

create inspire teach

WINTER ANSWER KEYS

Name: _____ ANSWER KEY

THE SNOWY ADVENTURE

    Once upon a wintery day in the little town of Pineville, four friends decided to go on an adventure. Wrapped up in scarves, hats, and puffy jackets, they trudged out into the white world, their boots leaving footprints behind them.

    Sam, the bravest, led the way with a map he'd drawn himself. Mia carried a backpack full of snacks and a thermos of hot cocoa. Leo had a camera to snap photos, and Zoe brought along her curiosity, which was just as important as anything you could pack.

    Their breath puffed out in frosty clouds as they made their way to the Whispering Woods, known for its tall trees and the way the wind whistled through the branches. Today, the woods were quiet, the trees standing like silent, snowy giants.

    As they hiked, they played games. They guessed the shapes of clouds and spotted animal tracks crisscrossing the path. They even made up stories about where the squirrels hurried to and why the rabbits hopped so fast.

    It was Mia who first spotted something strange: a <u>glittering</u> from a hillside not far off the path. "Look over there!" she pointed. The friends pushed through a bush and found a hidden cave, its entrance sparkling with ice crystals.

    They peeked inside. The cave was a palace of ice, with icicles hanging like chandeliers and walls that shimmered blue and purple. Sunlight streamed in from holes in the roof, turning the snow on the floor into a carpet of diamonds.

    The friends explored the cave, their voices echoing softly. Leo took pictures, Mia passed around cocoa, and Zoe found a rock with strange markings. It looked like a map or a drawing of the stars.

    "We're like explorers," Zoe said, her eyes wide with wonder.

    "We are explorers," Sam agreed. "And we've discovered our own secret treasure."

    They stayed until the sun began to fade, then made their way back home, promising to keep the secret of the ice cave just between them. But the memories of that day, of the laughter and the glittering ice, stayed with them long after winter had melted into spring.

    And sometimes, on clear nights, they'd look up at the stars and think of the cave and the sparkling snow, and they'd know that adventures could be found anywhere, even right in their own backyards.

1. Which of the following statements is true about "The Snowy Adventure"?
a) The story takes place in a busy city.
b) The friends found a palace filled with gold.
<u>c) The friends went on a hike and discovered an ice cave.</u>
d) Sam was scared of exploring the cave.

2. Using context clues from the story, what does 'treasure' most likely mean in this context?
a) A chest filled with gold and jewels
<u>b) A valuable discovery or experience</u>
c) A map leading to hidden riches
d) A collection of rare coins

3. Which character trait best describes Mia?
a) Fearful
b) Careful
<u>c) Adventurous</u>
d) Lazy

4. In the story, the word 'glittering' is used to describe the ice cave. Which word is a synonym for 'glittering'?
a) Dull
<u>b) Sparkling</u>
c) Dark
d) Smooth

create inspire teach

PROMPT: Describe the most important discovery made by the friends during their adventure in the Whispering Woods. ✓ checklist

Restate the question		The most important discovery made during their adventure in Whispering Woods **ANSWER KEY**	✓
Answer the question		was the ice cave.	✓
Cite evidence from the text	• According to the text, • The text says, • It is shown in the text,	The text says, The cave was a palace of ice, with icicles hanging like chandeliers and walls that shimmered blue and purple.	✓
Explain how the evidence proves your answer	• When I read___, I felt… • This part seems important because, • This part shows…	This part shows that this cave was amazing inside.	✓
Summarize	• Piecing everything together… • Drawing everything together… • The big lesson is…	Drawing everything together, it is clear to see that the most important discovery for the friends was the magical ice cave.	✓
	CAPITAL LETTER, PUNCTUATION MARKS, CORRECT SPELLING		✓

The most important discovery made during their adventure in Whispering Woods was the ice cave. The text says, The cave was a palace of ice, with icicles hanging like chandeliers and walls that shimmered blue and purple. This part shows that this cave was amazing inside. Drawing everything together, it is clear to see that the most important discovery for the friends was the magical ice cave.

create inspire teach

Name: _____ **ANSWER KEY**

THE MYSTERIOUS SNOWMAN

On a snowy lane in the cozy town of Evergreen, the children waited all year for the first snowfall. Not just for snowball fights or to sled down the big hill by Mr. McCreery's barn, but for a special tradition – building Mr. Frosty, their magnificent snowman.

This year, Mr. Frosty stood proudly in the center of the park, wearing a bright red scarf and a hat that wobbled in the wind. Carrot for a nose, coal for eyes, and a big, friendly smile made of pebbles – he was perfect. The children stood back and admired their work, high-fiving each other with mittened hands.

But the next morning, something strange had happened. Mr. Frosty had moved! Not much, just to the edge of the park, but it was enough to cause a flurry of excitement.

"Maybe he's alive," whispered Lily, her eyes wide with wonder.

"Or maybe someone is playing a trick on us," said Max, always the detective.

They decided to keep a watchful eye on Mr. Frosty. Each day, they took turns peeking out their windows, but the snowman only seemed to move when they looked away.

On the fourth morning, Mr. Frosty had moved again, this time next to the big oak tree. Near his new spot, they found a clue: birdseed scattered all around.

"Birds!" exclaimed Zoe. "Maybe they're pecking at the seeds and pushing Mr. Frosty around."

They tested their theory, placing seeds in one spot and watching from afar. Soon enough, a group of plump birds came fluttering down, eating eagerly. But Mr. Frosty didn't move.

The children scratched their heads, puzzled. It was a real winter mystery!

The answer came the next day when they saw Mr. Jasper, the park keeper, chuckling as he pushed Mr. Frosty back to the center of the park.

"You kids did such a fine job, I thought Mr. Frosty deserved the best spot in the park – right where everyone can see him!" he explained.

The children laughed. Their snowman hadn't walked on his own, but he had brought the whole neighborhood together in a bit of wintery fun.

And so, Mr. Frosty stayed in the park all winter, a jolly figure that reminded everyone of the playful mystery and the shared joy that the cold months could bring.

1. Put these events in the order that they happened by number them 1-4.

2	Mr. Frosty was moved next to the big oak tree.
1	The children built Mr. Frosty.
4	Mr. Jasper explained why he moved Mr. Frosty.
3	The children found birdseed around Mr. Frosty.

2. In the passage, find a synonym for 'puzzled':
a) Excited
b) <u>Confused</u>
c) Delighted
d) Scared

3. Imagine an illustration of children looking out their windows at Mr. Frosty. What might this picture suggest about the next part of the story?
a) They are planning to build another snowman.
b) <u>They are keeping a watchful eye on Mr. Frosty.</u>
c) They are about to go to school.
d) They are deciding to play elsewhere.

create inspire teach

PROMPT:	Why is this passage titled, "The Mysterious Snowman?"	✓ checklist
Restate the question	The passage was titled "The Mysterious Snowman" because **ANSWER KEY**	✓
Answer the question	the snowman moved without the kids knowing how.	✓
Cite evidence from the text	• One important moment from the story… • An example from the text is… • As stated in the text,	One important moment from the story was when the kids woke up and Mr. Frosty had moved to the edge of the park.	✓
Explain how the evidence proves your answer	• This evidence shows me, • This proves, • As you can see,	This evidence shows me that there was a mystery about the snowman.	✓
Summarize	• The text leaves us thinking about… • One thing is certain after reading… • Reflecting on the story…	One thing is certain, after reading this its important to remember that some things aren't what they seem.	✓
	CAPITAL LETTER, PUNCTUATION MARKS, CORRECT SPELLING	✓

The passage was titled "The Mysterious Snowman" because the snowman moved without the kids knowing how. One important moment from the story was when the kids woke up and Mr. Frosty had moved to the edge of the park. This evidence shows me that there was a mystery about the snowman. One thing is certain, after reading this its important to remember that some things aren't what they seem.

create inspire teach

Name: _____ ANSWER KEY

LUCY'S WINTER GARDEN

Lucy loved her garden. In spring, it bloomed with daffodils and tulips. In summer, it buzzed with bees around roses and sunflowers. In fall, it was full of red and gold leaves, but winter turned it into a sparkling wonderland, and that's when Lucy found it most <u>magical.</u>

One crisp winter morning, Lucy put on her warmest coat, a fuzzy hat, and mittens. She stepped outside, her boots crunching on the snow, and took a deep breath. The air was cold but fresh, and her garden was waiting.

She noticed the pond had turned to ice. The trees were bare, their branches covered in white. It looked like everything was asleep, but Lucy knew better. She had learned in school that even in winter, the garden was full of life.

She crouched down to inspect the bushes. Underneath, she saw tracks from rabbits and squirrels. "They must be looking for the nuts and berries I left out," she thought with a smile.

Next, she saw tiny footprints leading to a small hole. "That's where the field mice live," she whispered. "They stay warm under the snow."

Lucy filled the bird feeder, scattering seeds on the snow. Soon, her garden was filled with the flutter of wings and the songs of grateful birds.

Then, she made a surprising discovery. Beneath the snow, she found green shoots pushing up through the earth. "These must be the snowdrops," Lucy guessed. "They don't mind the cold at all!"

Lucy spent the whole afternoon in her winter garden, watching and learning. She saw that every plant and every creature had its way of handling the frosty days.

As the sky turned orange and pink, Lucy went back inside, her cheeks rosy from the cold. She sat by the window with a cup of hot cocoa, gazing out at her garden.

She realized that every season brought its own kind of beauty, even winter. And while the garden looked different under a blanket of snow, it was still full of life and little surprises.

That night, as Lucy snuggled under her blankets, she dreamed of her garden – not just as it was now, but as it would be in the spring, full of color and life once again.

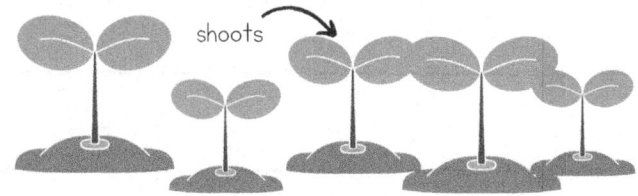
shoots

1. <u>Part A</u>: What does Lucy discover under the snow in her garden?
a) A buried treasure
<u>b) Green shoots of snowdrops</u>
c) A lost toy
d) An ice sculpture

<u>Part B</u>: Which sentence from the text supports your answer in Part A?
a) "She stepped outside, her boots crunching on the snow."
b) "Lucy filled the bird feeder, scattering seeds on the snow."
<u>c) "Beneath the snow, she found green shoots pushing up through the earth."</u>
d) "Lucy went back inside, her cheeks rosy from the cold."

2. In the passage, what does 'magical' most likely mean?
a) Something that involves magic or spells
<u>b) Causing a feeling of great surprise or wonder; enchanting</u>
c) Difficult to understand or explain
d) Something made by a magician

3. What is the effect of Lucy filling the bird feeder?
a) The birds stay away from her garden.
<u>b) The garden becomes filled with the flutter of wings and songs.</u>
c) The snow starts to melt.
d) The rabbits and squirrels come out of hiding.

create inspire teach

			✓ checklist
PROMPT:	What lessons about nature and the changing seasons does Lucy learn from her winter garden?		
Restate the question		The lesson that Lucy learns about nature and the changing seasons from her winter garden is that **ANSWER KEY**	✓
Answer the question		every season brought its own beauty to the garden.	✓
Cite evidence from the text	• (The character) says… • To support this idea, in paragraph ___, it says • A key detail from the text is…	To support this idea, in paragraph 1, it says in summer, it buzzed with bees around roses and sunflowers. In fall, it was full of red and gold leaves, but winter turned it into a sparkling wonderland.	✓
Explain how the evidence proves your answer	• I noticed… • Because of this, I think… • An interesting part is when…	Because of this, I think that Lucy loved every part of part of her garden throughout the different times of year.	✓
Summarize	• In the end, it's clear that… • Looking back, • It all comes down to…	In the end, it's clear that every season brought its own beauty to the garden.	✓
	CAPITAL LETTER, PUNCTUATION MARKS, CORRECT SPELLING		✓

The lesson that Lucy learns about nature and the changing seasons from her winter garden is that every season brought its own beauty to the garden. To support this idea, in paragraph 1, it says in summer, it buzzed with bees around roses and sunflowers. In fall, it was full of red and gold leaves, but winter turned it into a sparkling wonderland. Because of this, I think that Lucy loved every part of part of her garden throughout the different times of year. In the end, it's clear that every season brought its own beauty to the garden.

Name: _____ ANSWER KEY

THE COZY CABIN

Miles from the bustling city, nestled in a snowy forest clearing, stood a cozy cabin with smoke curling up from its chimney. This was the Winter family's cabin, and for Emma and her brother, Alex, it was the most magical place to be during winter break.

Their family had just arrived for the weekend. As they stepped out of the car, the crisp, pine-scented air greeted them, and the untouched snow sparkled. They rushed to the cabin, eager to see the familiar wooden walls and the old stone fireplace that was always the perfect place to warm cold fingers and toes.

After unpacking, Emma and Alex couldn't wait to explore. They pulled on their snow boots, wound scarves around their necks, and set out to make the most of the winter wonderland.

Their first stop was the hill behind the cabin, perfect for sledding. They took turns, shrieking with delight as they slid down the smooth, icy path they had created. After many runs and a couple of friendly snowball fights, they decided to build a snowman. They rolled big snowballs for the body and found rocks for eyes, a carrot for the nose, and sticks for arms. He was a great snowman.

As dusk fell, the temperature dropped, and the children headed inside, noses red and cheeks flushed from the cold. Inside, the cabin was warm and inviting. Their parents had started a fire, and the flames danced merrily in the fireplace.

That evening, they all sat by the fire, sipping hot chocolate and sharing stories. The cabin was filled with the sound of laughter and the comforting crackle of the firewood. Emma and Alex felt cozy and safe, wrapped in the soft glow of the firelight.

The next day brought more adventures. They found animal tracks in the snow and followed them, pretending to be explorers. They discovered a family of deer grazing quietly, and for a moment, everything was still.

Back at the cabin, their parents had made a warm, delicious meal. The family sat around the table, sharing their day's adventures and planning the next. There were more hills to sled down, more snowmen to build, and perhaps even ice-skating on the frozen pond nearby.

When the weekend came to an end, Emma and Alex were sad to leave the cabin. But as they drove away, they knew they would carry the warmth of the cabin with them, not just in their memories, but in their hearts, long after the snow had melted and the first blooms of spring had appeared.

The Cozy Cabin was more than just a place; it was a reminder that the simplest moments are the most precious.

1. <u>Part A</u>: What did Emma and Alex first do when they arrived at the cabin?
a) Built a snowman
b) Drank hot chocolate
<u>c) Went sledding</u>
d) Sat by the fireplace

<u>Part B</u>: Which sentence from the text supports your answer in Part A?
a) "They pulled on their snow boots, wound scarves around their necks, and set out to make the most of the winter wonderland."
b) "Inside, the cabin was warm and inviting."
c) "They rolled big snowballs for the body and found rocks for eyes, a carrot for the nose, and sticks for arms."
<u>d) "Their first stop was the hill behind the cabin, perfect for sledding."</u>

2. What does 'bustling' most likely mean in the context of the story?
a) Quiet and calm
<u>b) Busy and lively</u>
c) Slow and dull
d) Cold and snowy

create inspire teach

PROMPT: Why did Emma and Alex enjoy their time at the cabin? ✓ checklist

ANSWER KEY

Restate the question	Emma and Alex enjoyed their time at the cabin		✓
Answer the question	because they were able to go sledding, build a snowman, and sit by the fire with their family.		✓
Cite evidence from the text	• In the beginning/middle/end of the story, it mentions... • The narrator point out. • Drawing from the text.	In the end of the story, it mentions that Emma and Alex were sad to leave the cabin but they knew they would carry the warmth of the cabin with them.	✓
Explain how the evidence proves your answer	• This conversation shows... • What the characters did here tells us that... • From what I read, I know this is important because	From what I read, I know this is important because it shows that their time at the cabin was important to them.	✓
Summarize	• After reading the text, I realized... • Overall, the story teaches us... • All in all,	All in all, Emma and Alex enjoyed playing and spending time with their family while they were at their cabin.	✓
	CAPITAL LETTER, PUNCTUATION MARKS, CORRECT SPELLING		✓

Emma and Alex enjoyed their time at the cabin because they were able to go sledding, build a snowman, and sit by the fire with their family. In the end of the story , it mentions that Emma and Alex were sad to leave the cabin but they knew they would carry the warmth of the cabin with them. From what I read, I know this is important because it shows that their time at the cabin was important to them. All in all, Emma and Alex enjoyed playing and spending time with their family while they were at their cabin.

create inspire teach

Name: _____ ANSWER KEY

THE WINTER CARNIVAL AT SUNNYVALE SCHOOL

One chilly winter day, Sunnyvale School was buzzing with excitement. Today was the day of the Winter Carnival, and everyone was ready for fun!

The school was transformed into a winter wonderland. Colorful banners swayed in the breeze, and laughter filled the air. There were games like 'Snowball Toss' and 'Find the Penguin,' and a big slide made of snow!

Mrs. Lee's 2nd-grade class was in charge of the 'Hot Chocolate Stand.' Tommy, Sara, and their friends had worked together to set it up. They had big jugs of hot chocolate and piles of marshmallows.

"Remember, teamwork makes our stand the best!" Mrs. Lee reminded them with a smile.

At the snowball toss, children lined up to throw snowballs at targets. Each time someone hit the bullseye, everyone cheered. It didn't matter if it was a hit or a miss; everyone was having a great time.

Nearby, the 'Find the Penguin' game was a big hit. Children searched for hidden penguin toys around the playground. "I found one!" yelled Max, holding up a small toy penguin. His friends gathered around, clapping and laughing.

At the hot chocolate stand, Tommy and Sara worked together. Tommy poured the hot chocolate, and Sara added the marshmallows. "Teamwork is fun!" Sara said, giggling as she handed a cup to a little kindergartener.

As the day went on, children slid down the snow slide, laughing and squealing with joy. Even the teachers took turns, sliding down with big smiles.

The Winter Carnival wasn't just about winning games or drinking hot chocolate. It was about being together, helping each other, and enjoying the day as a community.

When the sun began to set, and the carnival came to an end, the children felt happy and tired. They had learned that working together and sharing joy made everything more fun.

As they left the schoolyard, the lights from the carnival twinkled like stars. They waved goodbye, already looking forward to next year's Winter Carnival.

That night, as the children of Sunnyvale School drifted off to sleep, they dreamt of snowflakes, laughter, and the warmth of friendship.

1. Put these events in the order that they happened by number them 1-4.

2	Tommy and Sara worked together at the Hot Chocolate Stand.
4	The children felt happy and tired at the end of the day.
1	The schoolyard was turned into a winter wonderland.
3	Children searched for hidden penguin toys.

2. What mood is created during the Winter Carnival?
a) Mysterious
<u>b) Exciting and joyful</u>
c) Scary
d) Sad

3. Imagine an illustration showing children playing the 'Snowball Toss' game. How does this image relate to the story?
a) It shows the competitive nature of the carnival.
<u>b) It reflects the fun and community spirit of the carnival.</u>
c) It indicates that the story is about sports.
d) It suggests that the carnival was held indoors.

PROMPT:	How did teamwork make the winter carnival successful?	✓ checklist
Restate the question	Team work made the winter festival successful ANSWER KEY	✓
Answer the question	because without the students working together, it wouldn't have been as fun.	✓
Cite evidence from the text	• A quote that shows this... • From the dialogue, it's clear that... • The author mentions...	A quote that shows this is when Mrs. Less said "Remember, teamwork makes our stand the best!"	✓
Explain how the evidence proves your answer	• This made me think of when... • It's interesting that the story says... • This part seems important because...	This part is important because all the kids worked together to run the games, and pass out the food and drinks.	✓
Summarize	• To sum it all up, • In conclusion, • Without a doubt,	Without a doubt, working together made the winter carnival a success!	✓
CAPITAL LETTER, PUNCTUATION MARKS, CORRECT SPELLING		✓

Team work made the winter festival successful because without the students working together, it wouldn't have been as fun. A quote that shows this is when Mrs. Less said "Remember, teamwork makes our stand the best!" This part is important because all the kids worked together to run the games, and pass out the food and drinks. Without a doubt, working together made the winter carnival a success!

Name: _____ **ANSWER KEY**

WINTER WONDERS: ANIMALS IN THE COLD

Did you know that animals have special ways to survive the cold winter? Let's explore some amazing winter adaptations!

Bears are famous for hibernating. When it gets cold, they find a cozy den and take a long sleep. Their heartbeats slow down, and they use their fat stores for energy. This way, they don't need to eat until spring!

Meanwhile, some birds, like geese, fly to warmer places. This journey is called <u>migration</u>. They travel long distances to find food and a warm habitat.

But what about the tiny squirrels? They don't hibernate or migrate. Instead, they collect nuts in the fall and hide them. During winter, they use these hidden treasures as their food supply.

Each of these animals has a special way to handle the chilly weather. While we bundle up in coats and scarves, they use their own amazing methods to enjoy the winter wonderland!

Geese are born with the instinct to migrate. They don't learn it from their parents; they are naturally programmed to know when and where to go.

1. <u>Part A</u>: What is the main idea of this passage?
a) Bears are the most interesting animals in winter.
<u>b) Different animals have unique ways to survive in winter.</u>
c) Squirrels are smarter than other animals in winter.
d) Birds migrate every season, not just in winter.

Part B: Which sentence from the passage best supports your answer to Part A?
a) "When it gets cold, bears find a cozy den and take a long sleep.
b) Birds travel long distances to find food and a warm habitat.
c) Squirrels use these hidden treasures as their food supply.
<u>d) Each of these animals has a special way to handle the chilly weather."</u>

2. What is the synonym of 'hibernating' as used in the passage?
<u>a) Sleeping</u>
b) Eating
c) Migrating
d) Playing

3. If there was a sidebar in the passage about 'migration,' what information would it most likely contain?
a) Different types of nuts squirrels eat.
b) The process of bears falling asleep.
<u>c) Why some birds fly to warmer places in winter.</u>
d) How animals play in the snow.

4. If you read another text about animals in summer, what detail would most likely be different compared to this passage?
a) Bears hibernating
b) Birds migrating
c) Squirrels storing food
<u>d) All of the above</u>

create inspire teach

PROMPT:	How do animals do to survive in the winter?		✓ checklist
Restate the question	To survive in the winter,	**ANSWER KEY**	✓
Answer the question	bears hibernate, birds migrate, and squirrels eat the food they had stored.		✓
Cite evidence from the text	• According to the text, • The text says, • It is shown in the text	The text says, bears heartbeats slow down, and they use their fat stores for energy. This way, they don't need to eat until spring!	✓
Explain how the evidence proves your answer	• This evidence shows me, • This proves, • As you can see,	This evidence shows me, that this is one way for animals to survive during the cold winter months.	✓
Summarize	• To sum it all up, • In conclusion, • Without a doubt,	In conclusion, all animals have specials ways of surviving during winter.	✓
	CAPITAL LETTER, PUNCTUATION MARKS, CORRECT SPELLING		✓

To survive in the winter, bears hibernate, birds migrate, and squirrels eat the food they had stored. The text says, bears heartbeats slow down, and they use their fat stores for energy. This way, they don't need to eat until spring! This evidence shows me, that this is one way for animals to survive during the cold winter months. In conclusion, all animals have specials ways of surviving during winter!

create inspire teach

Name: __ANSWER KEY__

THE SECRET WORLD OF SNOWFLAKES

Have you ever caught a snowflake on your glove and looked at its tiny, beautiful shape? Every snowflake is a small wonder of nature. Let's discover how they are made!

Snowflakes begin their life high up in the cold sky. When it's very cold, tiny drops of water in clouds freeze into ice crystals. As these crystals fall through the sky, they bump into each other and stick together. This journey is like a dance where they collect more and more tiny ice pieces.

The most amazing part is that each snowflake takes its own path. Because they travel different ways, they look different too. It's like each snowflake has its own story to tell. That's why no two snowflakes are exactly alike!

Some snowflakes might look like stars, others like tiny needles, and some even look like beautiful lace. So next time it snows, catch a flake and take a close look. You'll be holding a <u>unique</u> piece of winter's magic in your hand!

1. <u>Part A</u>: According to the passage, how are snowflakes formed?
a) From raindrops freezing in the sky.
b) By clouds moving in the sky.
<u>c) From tiny drops of water freezing into ice crystals in clouds.</u>
d) From snow falling and sticking together on the ground.

<u>Part B</u>: Which detail from the passage supports your answer in Part A?
a) "Every snowflake is a small wonder of nature."
<u>b) "Snowflakes begin their life high up in the cold sky."</u>
c) "Some snowflakes might look like stars, others like tiny needles."
d) "You'll be holding a unique piece of winter's magic in your hand."

2. What sequence best describes the formation of a snowflake as explained in the text?
<u>a) It freezes, falls, bumps into other crystals, sticks together.</u>
b) It bumps into other crystals, sticks together, freezes, falls.
c) It falls, bumps into other crystals, freezes, sticks together.
d) It sticks together, falls, bumps into other crystals, freezes.

3. What is an antonym of 'unique' as used in the passage?
a) Special
<u>b) Ordinary</u>
c) Beautiful
d) Rare

4. If you were to add a diagram to this passage, what would it most likely show?
a) How animals live in the snow.
<u>b) The process of a snowflake's formation.</u>
c) Different types of winter sports.
d) How to catch snowflakes on a glove.

create inspire teach

PROMPT: Why doesn't every snowflake look the same?   ✓ checklist

Restate the question	Snowflakes don't all look the same because		✓
		ANSWER KEY	
Answer the question	they go through a special process of freezing, falling and then bumping and sticking to each other as they fall to ground		✓
Cite evidence from the text	• In paragraph ___, it says… • An example from the text is… • As cited in the text,	As cited in the text, because snowflakes travel different ways, they look different.	✓
Explain how the evidence proves your answer	• Connecting this to the question, it's clear that • This part of the text reveals • This supports the idea because	This supports the idea that not all snowslakes look the same.	✓
Summarize	• The biggest idea here is • In short, • All in all,	All in all, snowflakes go through a special process as they fall to the Earth which makes them all look different.	✓
	CAPITAL LETTER, PUNCTUATION MARKS, CORRECT SPELLING		✓

Snowflakes don't all look the same because they go through a special process of freezing, falling and then bumping and sticking to each other as they fall to ground. As cited in the text, because snowflakes travel different ways, they look different. As cited in the text, because snowflakes travel different ways, they look different. This supports the idea that not all snowflakes look the same. All in all, snowflakes go through a special process as they fall to the Earth which makes them all look different.

create inspire teach

Name: _____ ANSWER KEY

WINTER HOLIDAYS AROUND THE WORLD

Winter is a time of joy and celebration around the globe. Different countries have unique holidays with exciting traditions!

In the United States, people celebrate Christmas by decorating trees and exchanging gifts. Families gather to share meals and enjoy the <u>festive</u> spirit.

Far away in India, there's a festival called Diwali. It's a festival of lights where people light lamps, set off fireworks, and eat delicious sweets. It symbolizes the victory of light over darkness.

In Mexico, families celebrate Las Posadas. For nine nights, they reenact Mary and Joseph's journey to Bethlehem with songs and processions. Piñatas filled with treats add fun to the celebration.

Hanukkah, a Jewish holiday, is celebrated with the lighting of the menorah, a special candle holder. Families enjoy games and foods fried in oil, like latkes and doughnuts.

Each of these holidays brings people together. They remind us of kindness, sharing, and the beauty of different cultures during the magical winter season.

1. <u>Part A</u>: What is a common theme in all the winter holidays mentioned in the passage?
a) Giving and receiving gifts.
b) Decorating homes and public places.
<u>c) Celebrating with food and traditions.</u>
d) Spending time outdoors in the snow.

<u>Part B:</u> Which holiday is celebrated with a specific activity for nine nights?
a) Christmas in the United States.
b) Diwali in India.
<u>c) Las Posadas in Mexico.</u>
d) Hanukkah.

3. What does 'festival' most closely mean in this context?
a) A large meal.
b) A religious ceremony.
<u>c) A celebration or gathering with special activities.</u>
d) A public speech or announcement.

4. If you read another text about summer holidays, what detail would most likely be different compared to this passage?
a) The type of celebrations.
b) The seasonal activities.
c) The cultural significance of the holidays.
<u>d) All of the above.</u>

create inspire teach

PROMPT:	What are some winter holidays celebrated around the world, and how are they celebrated?			✓ checklist
Restate the question	Some of the winter holidays that are celebrated around the world are		ANSWER KEY	✓
Answer the question	Christmas, Diwali, Las Posadas, and Hanukkah. They are celebrated in different ways, but most involve special foods.			✓
Cite evidence from the text	• The author shows that... • A quote that stands out is... • As evidence, the passage says...	The author shows that, during Diwali they eat delicious sweets and during Hanukkah they eat foods friend in oil.		✓
Explain how the evidence proves your answer	• Drawing conclusions from this, I can see that... • By stating this, the author is suggesting... • This is important because	This is important because it shows how different holidays are celebrated around the world.		✓
Summarize	• After reading, I think... • Breaking it down, • The gist of this passage...	The gist of this passage is that holidays are celebrated differently in different places.		✓
	CAPITAL LETTER, PUNCTUATION MARKS, CORRECT SPELLING			✓

Some of the winter holidays that are celebrated around the world are Christmas, Diwali, Las Posadas, and Hanukkah. They are celebrated in different ways, but most involve special foods. The author shows that, during Diwali they eat delicious sweets and during Hanukkah they eat foods friend in oil. This is important because it shows how different holodays are celebrated around the world. The gist of this passage is that holidays are celebrated differently in different places.

Name: _____ **ANSWER KEY**

WINTER SPORTS FUN

Winter is a season of fun and games, especially with winter sports! Have you ever watched skiing, snowboarding, or ice skating? These sports are not just exciting to watch but also <u>thrilling</u> to play.

Skiing is a sport where people slide down snowy hills on skis. It has been around for thousands of years. Originally, skis were used to travel over snow in cold countries. Now, skiing is a popular winter sport all over the world.

Snowboarding is like skiing, but instead of two skis, you use one big board. Did you know snowboarding started in the 1960s? It was inspired by surfing and skateboarding. People loved the idea of surfing on snow!

Ice skating is gliding on ice with skates. It's been around for centuries and began as a way to move across frozen lakes and rivers. Today, ice skating is a favorite winter activity. Some people even dance on ice!

Each of these sports is special. They remind us of the joy and excitement of winter. Maybe one day, you'll try one of them too!

1. <u>Part A</u>: What is the main idea of the passage?
a) Ice skating is the oldest winter sport.
<u>b) Winter sports include skiing, snowboarding, and ice skating.</u>
c) Snowboarding is the most popular winter sport.
d) Winter is the only time to play sports.

<u>Part B</u>: Which detail from the passage supports your answer in Part A?
a) "Skiing is a sport where people slide down snowy hills on skis."
b) "Snowboarding started in the 1960s."
c) "Ice skating is gliding on ice with skates."
<u>d) "Each of these sports is special."</u>

2. Match the winter sport with its historical origin:

3. What is the synonym of 'thrilling' as used in the passage?
a) Scary
<u>b) Exciting</u>
c) Slow
d) Boring

4. What effect did the invention of snowboarding have on winter sports?
a) It made skiing less popular.
<u>b) It added a new, exciting option inspired by surfing and skateboarding.</u>
c) It replaced ice skating.
d) It changed the way skiing was performed.

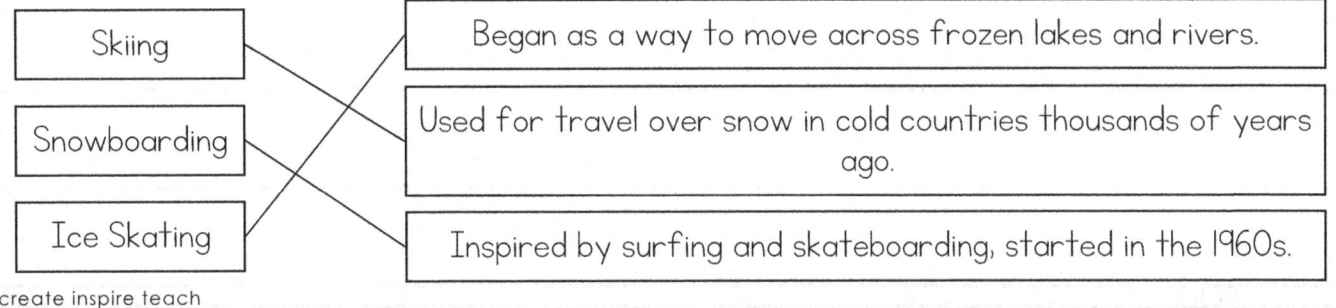

create inspire teach

PROMPT: Explain how winter sports like skiing, snowboarding, and ice skating have changed over time.

✓ checklist

ANSWER KEY

Restate the question	Winter sports have changed over time.		✓
Answer the question	Skiing, for example, was started as a way to travel over snow in cold countries.		✓
Cite evidence from the text	• Highlighting this point, the text states... • From the text we can see... • Supporting this idea, the text describes...	Supporting this idea, the text describes that skiing is now a popular winter sport done all over the world.	✓
Explain how the evidence proves your answer	• Because of this, I think • Putting this another way • This backs up my idea that	This backs up my idea that skiing went from a way to get from place to place to something people do for fun.	✓
Summarize	• Bringing everything together, • To summarize my thoughts • After breaking it down,	Bringing everything together, winter sports have changed over time.	✓
	CAPITAL LETTER, PUNCTUATION MARKS, CORRECT SPELLING		✓

Winter sports have changed over time. Skiing, for example, was started as a way to travel over snow in cold countries. Supporting this idea, the text describes that skiing is now a popular winter sport done all over the world. This backs up my idea that skiing went from a way to get from place to place to something people do for fun. Bringing everything together, winter sports have changed over time.

create inspire teach

Name: __ANSWER KEY__

THE DANCING LIGHTS OF THE NORTH

Have you ever seen pictures of bright, colorful lights in the night sky? Those are the Aurora Borealis, also known as the Northern Lights. They look like magical ribbons waving in the sky. But what causes these beautiful lights?

The sun sends out tiny particles that travel through space. When these particles reach the Earth, they meet our planet's magnetic field. The North and South Poles have strong magnetic forces. So, these particles are pulled towards them. When these particles from the sun touch the gases in the Earth's atmosphere, they light up! It's like nature's own light show!

The colors of the Northern Lights can be green, pink, purple, blue, and even red. They dance in the sky, especially during long, dark nights. The best places to see them is near the North Pole, in countries like Canada, Norway, and Iceland. People travel from all over the world to see this display. The Northern Lights remind us how beautiful and mysterious our planet can be.

1. Part A: What is the main idea of this passage?
<u>a) The Northern Lights are a light show caused by the sun's particles.</u>
b) The Northern Lights can only be seen in Canada, Norway, and Iceland.
c) The Northern Lights are always green in color.
d) The sun is the only star that affects Earth.

Part B: Which detail from the passage supports your answer in Part A?
a) "They look like magical ribbons waving in the sky."
<u>b) "When these particles from the sun touch the gases in the Earth's atmosphere, they light up!"</u>
c) "The best places to see them are near the North Pole."
d) "They dance in the sky, especially during long, dark nights."

3. How do the Northern Lights form, according to the passage?
a) The Earth's atmosphere creates them on its own.
<u>b) The sun's particles reach Earth and light up when they touch atmospheric gases.</u>
c) They are caused by the moon reflecting light.
d) They appear when it snows in the North Pole.

4. What is the meaning of 'particles' as used in the passage?
a) Animals
b) Plants
<u>c) Small pieces or bits</u>
d) Large objects

5. If the passage included a map, what would it most likely show?
<u>a) Locations where the Northern Lights can be seen</u>
b) Different countries in the world.
c) The sun and its particles.
d) Animals found near the North Pole.

create inspire teach

PROMPT:	Where and how does the Aurora Borealis happen?		✓ checklist
Restate the question	The Aurora Borealis happen when	**ANSWER KEY**	✓
Answer the question	particles from the sun touch the gases in the Earth's atmosphere.		✓
Cite evidence from the text	• The author states... • In the passage, it mentioned that... • From the reading, I learned...	The author states that the particles from the sun are pulled towards the north because the north pole has a strong magenetic forces.	✓
Explain how the evidence proves your answer	• This demonstrates that • From this, we can understand that • This detail shed light on	From this we can understand why the northern lights are only able to be seen in places near the North Pole in places like Canada, Norway, and Iceland.	✓
Summarize	• In a nutshell, • After reading, I know... • The main thing to remember	In a nutshell, the Aurora Borealis can be seen in places close to the North Pole and happens because of the particles from the sun touch the gases from the Earth's atmosphere.	✓
	CAPITAL LETTER, PUNCTUATION MARKS, CORRECT SPELLING		✓

The Aurora Borealis happen when particles from the sun touch the gases in the Earth's atmosphere. The author states that the particles from the sun are pulled towards the north because the north pole has a strong magenetic forces. From this we can understand why the northern lights are only able to be seen in places near the North Pole in places like Canada, Norway, and Iceland. In a nutshell, the Aurora Borealis can be seen in places close to the North Pole and happens because of the particles from the sun touch the gases from the Earth's atmosphere.

create inspire teach

Courtney Bluem
create ♥ inspire ♥ teach

THANK YOU FOR YOUR PURCHASE!

Want access to free resources?
CHECK OUT THE FREE RESOURCE LIBRARY!
createinspireteach.com/freebies

You May Also Like:

This workbook teaches students to develop constructed response paragraphs using the RACES writing strategy. With highly engaging and interesting passages, students will learn to use relevant text evidence to respond to an open-ended prompt. They will practice this skill with both fiction and nonfiction texts.

Terms of Use
Copyright 2023 Courtney Bluem. All rights reserved. By purchasing this product, you, the purchaser, are granted the right to reproduce pages for one person only. Duplication for more than one person or sharing with another person, grade level, school or district is strictly forbidden without written permission from the author.

Credits:

create inspire teach

Made in the USA
Las Vegas, NV
12 March 2025